Blueprints for Success

Networking

150 Ways to Promote Yourself

Bette Daoust, Ph.D.

Blueprint Books ™
Blueprints for Success

Pleasanton, California

A Penmarin Book

Copyright

A Penmarin Book
Roseville, California 95661
Phone: 916-771-5869
Fax: 916-771-5879

E-mail:
General Comments: penmarin@penmarin.com
Production: connie@penmarin.com
Editorial: ginny@penmarin.com
Marketing, Ordering, Pricing: hal@penmarin.com

Published by Blueprint Books
Post Office Box 10757
Pleasanton, CA 94588 USA

orders@BlueprintBooks.com
http://BlueprintBooks.com

For bookstore and library orders:
Midpoint Trade Books
27 W. 20th Street, Suite 1102
New York, NY 10011
(212) 727-0190
www.midpointtrade.com

Unattributed quotations are by Bette Daoust, Ph.D.
ISBN 1-883955-48-3
First printing 2005
Printed in the United States of America

Library of Congress Control Number: 2005921524

Table of Contents

About the Author

Bette Daoust, Ph.D. has been networking with others since leaving high school years ago. She realized that no one would really care about what she did in life unless she told people and excited them about her ideas. She decided to find the best ways to get people's attention, to be creative in how she presented herself and products, to get people to know who she was, and to be visible all the time. Her friends and colleagues have often dubbed her the "Networking Queen."

Several years ago, Dr. Daoust decided that she should keep track of all the things she was doing in order to let people know about her and her products. She decided to put into the mix her integrity, honesty, and drive to be successful. Continuing in this vein, she has used her writing skills from the publication of over 150 books, articles, white papers, and training guides to create a new series of books that will help others achieve business success. The Blueprints for Success Business Series was born.

This book, **Networking: 150 Ways to Promote Yourself**, is the first in this series. If you enjoy this book, you will certainly want to read the next one: **Branding Yourself: Another 150 Ways to Promote Yourself**, which is planned for release in late 2005.

Bette has an eclectic background in education, technology, and enterprise administration. She has worked with such companies as Peet's Coffee & Tea, Accenture, Avaya, and many others. Her Ph.D. is in Business Management from Northcentral University in Prescott Arizona. She is a former President of the Fort Langley Chamber of Commerce, past president of the Rotary Club of Langley Sunrise, past president of VISTA, District Historian for Rotary District 5170, and sits on the Board of Directors of other professional associations.

Dr. Daoust's true love is in sharing information with others and helping any business achieve a greater success.

WARNING-DISCLAIMER

This book is designed to provide information on networking, partnering with others, and forming alliances. It is sold with the understanding that the publisher and author are not engaged in rendering legal, accounting, or other professional services. If legal or other expert assistance is required, the services of a competent professional should be sought.

It is not the purpose of the book to reprint all the information that is otherwise available to networkers, but instead to complement, amplify and supplement other works. You are urged to read other materials on networking and put the information to personal use. See our Resource Guide for more books and information on where and how to network for success.

Networking does not provide you with a get-rich-quick scheme for acquiring new business. It does, however, provide some guidance as to where best to spend your time. You should make sure that you read other materials on the same subject and come up with your own personal networking plan.

Every effort has been made to make this book as accurate as possible. However, there *may be mistakes*, both typographical and in content. Therefore, this text should be used only as a general guide and not as the ultimate source of networking information. Furthermore, this book contains information on networking that is current only up to the printing date.

The purpose of this book is to educate and entertain. The author, Blueprint Books, and Penmarin Books shall have neither liability nor responsibility to any person or entity with respect to any loss or damage caused, or alleged to have been caused, directly or indirectly, by the information contained in this book.

If you do not wish to be bound by the above, you may return this book to the publisher for a full refund.

ACKNOWLEDGEMENTS

This book is the culmination of experiences of not only the author but of many business people whom she has surrounded herself with over the years. Every event has given inspiration as to what works and what does not.

Of all the people who have worked on this project, I would like to give kudos to my husband, François Daoust, for all the tireless hours spent editing, working on the book's Web presence, and putting the technological components together. I also want to thank both my daughters: Maren Grace for her editing and comments, and Carina Gilbert for her quickness in putting documentation together. Finally, thanks to Jim Fagan for his editing expertise, Kevin Gleason for his professional editing, and to Ronda Henstorf and Riley Design Associates for their creative ideas and production of the book covers.

I also want to thank my dear friend Jill Lublin for her support throughout this process. She has encouraged me to make sure my work is well publicized.

Without these people, none of this would be possible. My very sincere thanks to each of you.

Foreword

We often find ourselves sitting at our desks wondering how we will be able to contact enough people in order to push our product or service. Searching through the mire of networking groups and professional associations, getting to know people who know those you want to know, and simply standing in line at a grocery store take a great deal of time and effort. Often the effort is not as fine-tuned as we would like it to be and the searching, meeting, and greeting are not taking us as far as we would like to go. Some people tell us that contact through electronic means is the only way to go and others say that "meet and greet" is the best. Whichever way we decide to go may not always bring us to the destination we desire.

We have to learn that being honest with ourselves and believing in what we have to offer is the key to success when forming a business relationship. Networking is not about manipulating your audience so that they buy from you; it is about giving what you can to the other person without thought of personal gain. You have probably heard the saying "you get what you give." Taken into perspective, if you give to others, they will know who you are and share it with their contacts. You will become known by those you wish to meet. In reality, "it is who knows you" that counts and not "who you know."

Networking: 150 Ways to Promote Yourself will help you to weed through places that are not getting you the results you desire. By capitalizing on the years of experience from Dr. Bette Daoust, you will be able to save yourself time and money. This is the book that will help you make the right connections through the best organizations to make you and your business a success.

——Jill Lublin, author of the best sellers *Guerrilla Publicity* and *Networking Magic*, CEO of the strategic consulting firm Promising Promotion, and founder of GoodNews Media, Inc.

Introduction

One of my observations when I attend events is that people tend to talk only to those people they already know. People seem to really enjoy their own comfort zone, and straying far from that is a real chore and taps into personal "fear factors." It is not that we fear each other; we often fear rejection and what others will say about us when we are not around. It is my hope that this book, **Networking: 150 Ways to Promote Yourself**, will help you to get past your fear and start mingling with others and make a profit.

The book is divided into ten chapters plus a robust Resource Guide. The chapters will give you insights on how to better deal with networking events, form strategic alliances, work with your focus, utilize print and online media, and be a better purveyor of your business message.

The Resource Guide contains information that will help you further develop your networking circle. The resources include listings of books, leads exchanges, associations, networking opportunities, and service organizations. If anything, the Resource Guide will be one of the best used portions of this book.

I hope you will find our **Networking: 150 Ways to Promote Yourself** a valuable working tool.

Bette Daoust, Ph.D.
Chief Knowledge Officer,
BizMechanix.com

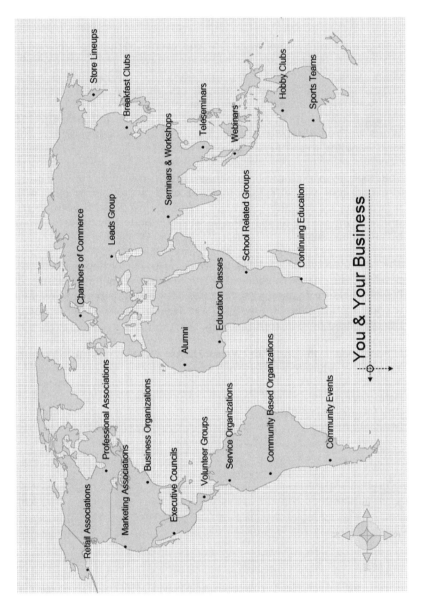

Networking Opportunities

1. Event Marketing

1. Don't Be All Things

> When people tell me that they do all of that plus whatever comes their way for business, why do I wonder what their expertise really is?

Have you ever been at a networking event and talked to someone about what he or she does? I have many times, and I am often quite amazed by the total range of services that some people offer the public. This practice is not unusual for a small business, but I begin to wonder what their focus is and I also wonder what their expertise is. I think such people don't realize that what they are doing is not good for their business.

Can you imagine doing business with someone who does your photocopying, gives talks about leadership, *and* shines your shoes? This may be called a one-stop shop, but what does the buying business expect to gain from this type of relationship? I certainly am leery about that kind of business. It seems like the person doing the selling will do anything just to get business. They attend every networking event they possibly can and "spray and pray," dragging along some unsuspecting soul to gain a business relationship. Does the unsuspecting soul have any idea that this person is one thing to her and is an entirely different person to another prospective business?

For example, I know a person who says she does sales training and also teaches businesses how to market their products. Her claim seems quite innocent until you dig a little and find out that her real expertise is in sales and not in marketing, two widely different fields in most people's minds. However, to continue the story, this person also offers leadership training, change management consulting, writing skills, and the list goes on. She also purports to be a professional speaker who will talk on any subject you give her.

When you move from spray and pray to a more focused approach, it is much easier to work with potential customers. You are moving from being everything with no expertise into a person who has something valuable to offer. Having focus gives you the ability to define your services and products in a more targeted manner. Plus, it will enable you to define your best customer according to your best services.

2. Define Your Best Customer

Why must you be able to describe the best possible
customer you could have for your business?

To be more effective at developing relationships, you should always take time to describe your best customer. This is the customer that gives you the biggest bang for your buck. This customer pays its bills on time and uses you exclusively for all its business needs in your area of expertise. It is also a customer that you have an excellent working relationship with. Its representatives know they can rely on you for the services you specialize in and that you will go out of your way to make sure that they are happy at all times. And if they are not happy, they know they can rely on you to analyze the problem, and come to a win-win solution for them.

This customer is the one that knows you are the best solution to its business pain. You are the one to help it pass through troubled times and come out the other end more profitable (as are you at the same time). This relationship will develop with ease and not take long periods of time to gel. This is the customer on which you can focus your energies and be able to help them focus on their core competencies at all times.

Since the customer that is best for you is also the customer that is best for another competitor, you must nurture this customer and not hang it out to dry. It is important that you have a process in place that allows you to make sure this customer is always happy.

For example, one day I came across a small human resources company that specialized in sales personnel. The company was working with many types of clients but found that certain clients brought in more money than others. The company decided to profile its best customers. Using the profile, it then concentrated its sales and marketing efforts on the potential customers that fit the profile. The result of this selectivity was that for the same effort the company made more money by not wasting time on clients that did not pay off.

Now that you know who your best customer is, you should look more closely at how you describe what you do best. The words that you choose to describe your business need to be very few and to the point—which is why such a description is often called an elevator pitch. The pitch also needs to be worded so that your identified best customer can easily understand what you do and how you can help them.

3. Your Pitch

Why should you describe your
business to others in 5 to 10 seconds?

How much time do you think you have to get anyone's attention? 5 minutes? 2 minutes? 30 seconds? It is actually 10 seconds. I know it does not seem like much time, but you will be amazed what you can say in 10 seconds. It is enough time to put your foot in your mouth and then try to get it out again. It is also enough to tell someone your expertise and have the person smiling and wanting to converse about it. This, of course, is what you want to happen. And you can put together the pitch so that it is a virtual guarantee.

First of all, you need to gain the interest of the prospect you are talking with, then you want them to be receptive to establishing a relationship and feel an interest in your product. Is it that difficult to put your best foot forward and get them interested? Of course not! Start by simplifying your message: Write down your core competencies, then describe them to the customer. Keep the customer in mind. Ask yourself, why would someone want to buy from you? Then tell them why! Put yourself in your customers' shoes (so to speak) and see what is in it for them.

This can all be accomplished in just a few seconds—your prospect may even have time to respond to you. Just make sure that you know what you are talking about. There is nothing worse than putting your best foot forward and tripping over your tongue. We will deal with how to practice in the next section. For now just follow the simple rules:

- ✓ Define your core competency.

- ✓ Describe that competency in laypersons' terms.

- ✓ Put it in writing and see how long it takes to say.

Have you ever watched another person practice a pitch? Not likely! Most people do not practice—they prefer to wing it and see what happens. If you take the time to memorize the pitch and make it a part of you and what you do, you will likely win more customers. It will also be received as more sincere and more believable. You need to pull out that mirror and get the camera rolling to see what you look like and how you can make improvements.

4. Practice Makes Perfect

How can you expect to be effective
if you do not practice your pitch?

Have you ever gone to a networking event and the person next to you is trying to describe what he does but he keeps miscuing the words? This happens so often at these events. The major problem, besides lack of focus, is that he has not practiced his spiel. Why don't people practice? Quite often you feel self-conscious trying to practice in front of a mirror when others are around to hear you try over and over again. The solution is to make sure you have a door closed so you cannot be disturbed. Or you may decide to audio- or videotape yourself to hear and see how you look while making the presentation.

This is how the professionals do it. They practice and practice until their presentation is smooth. Did you know that Robin Williams does at least 37 "takes" of any movie scene before he feels that his performance is up to par? He is a seasoned pro, yet he still practices all the time. Could you imagine Michael Jordan not practicing throwing balls into the hoop?

When you reach the professional level, practice becomes more imperative. Without practice, it is difficult to move forward; you will be surprised that the words do not flow the way they should. You must become the expert if you are to work a room effectively. Do not think of this in terms of a smooth-talking salesman (the connotation is often negative), but as the way you present yourself, with confidence and poise. People will more likely enjoy listening to you when your message is practiced and your delivery is smooth.

Practice is like acting: You need to keep working on it until you think the pitch is perfect. Practicing the words is not the only thing you need to work on. How you move your body, your eye contact, hand gestures, arm positions, how you stand, and your face looks, all must be mastered in your practice sessions. You need to treat your practice session as if you are playing a part in a movie. "Soft skills" such as body language and intonation all contribute to the pitch.

5. Soft Skills

Why are communication through body language
and appropriate language
crucial to a networking success?

Most people take quick note of someone who has an attitude—a person who acts belligerent, like a know-it-all, and whose ego sticks out like a sore thumb. This is not the kind of person you generally want to do business with. That goes for language as well: You do not want to hang with someone who is negative, always plays the victim, and is always whining about one thing or another.

That the way a person is speaking has an effect on listeners is pretty clear, but what may not be so evident is the effect of the listener's body language on the speaker. The fact that body language can work for you if you take time to listen to others is really important. The act of listening changes your body language almost immediately. So that you can understand what the other person is saying, you change from aggressive mode to passive mode. This type of body language makes others receptive to you, and they will want to tell their story to you.

However, when others want to tell their story, it is important that you gently nudge them in the right direction. You want them to tell you about their business pain, or what is not right with their company. It is through analyzing what they are saying that you will gain deeper insights as to what needs to be remedied and how you can help them with that part of their business. After all, you are at the event to pick up solid leads that will give you both profit and relationships that will last for quite some time. What about language? The kind of language you should be using is, "Will you . . . ?" "Have you considered . . . ?" "I'll find out how I can help," "I know someone who . . ."—even reiterating what they just said is good.

You have now practiced and rehearsed, done the dress rehearsal, filmed yourself, done the critique, worked with your director (yourself), and you have finally perfected the pitch. It is now time to try it on a live audience of real people. The first thing is to make sure you have chosen the right event to attend and next that what you are pitching is appropriate for the audience at that event. In the next section we will talk about choosing the appropriate event.

6. Which Events to Attend

Where do you look for your best prospects?

Customers are not a dime a dozen, especially in today's economy. For this reason, before deciding whether to attend an event, you should follow the rules given above for defining your best prospective customer. Is the event one that such a customer will attend? Customers have their preferences among events just as you do. They are also looking for ways to meet others. If you find out where your ideal customer goes, you should make a point of attending.

I have often gone to events that I would not normally attend, just to get close to a potential customer, and of course a potential sale. And you may meet someone completely unexpected at such an event. If your best customer profile attends this event, you can bet that others just like that profile will also be in attendance. In the long run, you will enhance your opportunity to capitalize on the event by being very discerning about who will be there. It is similar to the way you choose parties to attend in your personal life.

No need to do this with an attitude, but you need to be aware of where you should go and why. Not all events will fill the bill. For example, if you were selling high-end networking systems, you would not likely attend a Chamber of Commerce event for small business. Not that the Chamber does not have anything to offer, it is just that your best customer is not likely to attend such an event—though people who attend Chamber events may be connected to your best customer. Nevertheless, you will likely want to attend a business symposium directed at the larger corporations. They are more likely to attend events that other like-minded companies will also attend.

Events to attend will be one of the components of your calendar that you need to keep up to date at all times. Consistently attending events will allow others to get to know you better, even if it is only face recognition at first. When people know that you are always around, they are more likely to talk to you and find out more. It is a great feeling when someone comes up to you and says, "How are you doing? How is business going? Let's chat."

7. Plan Ahead

> To make the best of an event,
> plan to eat early, then network!

Have you ever attended an event and seen all the people gravitating toward the food and the drinks? These amenities are the first thing people seem to go for. Well, it is natural, especially if you are there alone and do not know anyone. The food and drink seem to be there for comfort. However, it is really difficult to talk with your mouth full, so if you can, stay away from the food, but certainly go and get a drink. You can still give your pitch with a drink in hand. Remember to eat first (go early to the event) and then Network!

Before you head off to an event, take a look at your calendar. This is part of the preparation you need to do beforehand. You will need to know from memory when you are free for a follow-up appointment. Then you can make a date and know there is no conflict with other items on your calendar. Nothing is worse than setting an appointment and finding out that you already have scheduled someone else in that time slot. It may seem like a good excuse for a follow-up, but it usually does not bode well with a potential client.

You do not want to partake of any conversation with someone who is whining about some guy that can never get anything straight. Just remember that you are at the event for one purpose and one purpose only—to gain new business relationships and be as visible as possible. You should also work on techniques for easing politely into private conversations without interrupting the flow of information; barging in and being rude—however accidentally—will not serve your purpose.

Have you ever gone to an event and not worn the correct attire? Part of planning for an event (seeing who will be attending) is to also research the nature of the event. Does the weather have an effect on who attends? Does the required dress have an effect on where it is held? Who will be leading the event and how are they regarded? What attitude does the event portray? It all comes down to knowing your audience and researching the event before you attend.

8. Know the Audience

What is worse than wearing a tuxedo to an event
when everyone else is attending in shorts?

I have said the same thing over and over again: Before you attend an event, get to know the audience. If the audience is not right for you, you may attend, but knowing you are unlikely to gain any new business. If, on the other hand, you want to attend just to form new relationships with others in the business community, by all means do so. Just do not stretch yourself so thin that another event will topple you. So, the first thing you must do before attending is to find out who will be there. If there is someone specific you want to meet, then find someone who knows her and get a proper introduction.

A third party introduction will go a lot farther than just introducing yourself from left field. Introductions have a way of confirming that you are worth knowing. Remember, the person you meet should be the one who makes the decisions for his company. I am not saying you should not form relationships with influencers—just the opposite; but it is best if your first relationship is with the decision maker. If this is not possible, then getting to know about the company through others is a good way to understand the processes for obtaining business. These individuals often will introduce you to the person who makes the decisions. This type of third party introduction works wonders.

Make sure you know exactly who will be attending the events and then find out their status within the company. The size of the company may matter to you, so make sure you know its size before making any approaches. It is often said that it is not who you know but who knows you that counts. When a company needs someone with your skill set and they know who you are, it is likely you are the one who will be contacted for business. Most people like to show they are well connected in the community.

You have now discovered who is attending the event and perhaps even why they are there. Most often you will find that attendees are there to get more business. Sometimes they may be there to hear the speaker, who is often the draw. Once you have the audience analyzed, you need to prepare not only your pitch, but also the questions you need to ask to get the answers you are looking for.

9. Questions to Ask

What can you ask someone
to find out his or her business problems?

We define "business pain" as a problem that a business needs to solve. The pain may be that they do not have enough sales, or they do not have an appropriate process for tracking their forecasting. The pain could even be that they cannot hire the appropriate staff in order the handle daily requirements. Most often when you are at an event, business people talk about what is bothering them at work. They do not talk about their successes (especially if they are being overheard) and they do not talk about other wins. They will talk about their pain. It is through asking questions that you will find out what that pain is.

One good question is always, "How are your sales doing this quarter?" or this year. You may also ask them what they are currently working on to improve their business processes. There are a host of other questions you can ask in order to get the answers you are looking for. When asking questions, do not get into specifics; you need to generalize because you want to make the appointment to go deeper into what their company does. The goal of diving into the business pain is not to find out what the pain is per se, it is to find out that there is pain and in what areas.

If you are specifically interested in sales, then the questions should generally be directed around sales and not, say, the HR questions. You must be specific about what you want to know and not what the person is leading you toward. There is often pain in more than one area of a business.

Now that you have asked all the important questions, you will receive the answers. These may not always be the ones you are looking for; it may be that you have no chance at doing business with this person. The important thing is to make sure that you listen carefully to what she has to say. You should not take notes, as it is distracting to the speaker; spend time practicing your listening skills.

10.Listen, Listen, Listen

How do you learn anything about the other person's business if you do not spend most of your time listening to what he has to say?

I cannot say it enough: Always listen and do not try to interrupt what others are saying. The less you talk, the more information you will gather about the other person's business. It is also important that you jot the info down as soon as you leave the conversation. We will go into this a little later in the book. Getting back to listening— you must tune yourself into key words so that you will know if this is a person you want to do business with.

Key words are what you are listening for, not the general conversation topics. General conversation does not usually lead to specifics as to the exact pain; you need to interject and ask a few questions, and then keep on listening. What matters is not what you have to say but what you ask and how you listen to the answers. Be sure you hang on every word for the message you are looking for— even offer some temporary solutions that you can follow up with at a later appointment. Listening is the key to all business relationships; you must practice this skill over and over.

It is not an easy task to constantly listen and not beat your own drum. Did you ever go to a party where all people talked about was themselves? You will likely find that you fall into this category as well. We have a natural tendency to talk about ourselves and not really listen to what others have to say. Another important point is not to start talking at the same time as the other person; he will find it annoying as he has not had a chance to finish talking (about himself, of course).

Listening is a skill that needs to be practiced. It is very difficult to hear others talk and not make comments. You should practice listening with a partner. Take a timer and plan for 5 minutes of listening before you speak. Have your partner talk about her life story while you simply listen. This is probably one of the most difficult things to do; you need to practice patience while listening to others.

11.Practice Patience

If it is very natural for people to talk about
themselves and their business,
how can you be patient and slip a salient point in
to solve someone else's problems?

Patience is a virtue. Without patience we would move at breakneck speed without taking time to reflect on others' thoughts and words. To really understand what they have said, we have to first spend time listening, and then we must practice patience before talking ourselves, taking time to assimilate what was said. Listening patiently also means waiting until they have finished talking. It can be very annoying when a person goes on and on. This person is likely not aware that he is boring those around him, and that he is, as we say, "sucking all the oxygen out of the room." But if you take time to really listen to what he has to say, you may learn something new. In this situation, it is best to allow the person to talk while interjecting a question now and then.

It may seem like you are egging him on (and in a way you are), but in reality you are practicing patience by allowing him to talk with you, steering him in the direction you would like him to go. Even as he is talking, you should be making mental notes about the topic— especially if it has to do with some business pain that your company can solve for him. Being patient is probably one of the most difficult things to do, but it has its own rewards for the listener. Just think about a time when you waited in line and ended up being the last one served just before the teller closed and there were some left over goodies for you to take. The patience paid off.

So you have asked the questions, spent your time listening to the other person, and secretly taken mental notes on the answers. Now it is time to decide whether there is a possibility of doing business with this person. If so, it is not a simple question of asking for a meeting, and definitely not simply collecting his business card. Timing is everything, and this is about timing the best way to exchange information.

12. How to Collect Cards

The business card grab is not why you are there.
So how do you obtain the card
and show interest that gains confidence?

Two questions I am always asked is, "How do you collect cards?" and "What do you do with them when you get them back to the office?" What really happens when you collect business cards? Often they get put into a pocket with many others. Have you ever collected cards to later find out that you have no idea who the person who gave you a certain card was? This happens all the time. Some people look at their stack of cards the next day or, even worse, two days later and are bewildered: they can't remember who was who.

It is probably better to pick a few good leads rather than collect every card (sometimes that is difficult to avoid if people trade cards with you). It is quite easy to cull the cards as you gather them. First, I collect cards only from people with whom I can either do business or form an alliance, or for whom I simply become a referral. Sounds easy, but the trick is to be able to ferret out who these people are.

Choose one pocket for the timely leads and carry Post-it notes to add information. Cards with simple black and white designs can look very alike; it is very important that you try to differentiate the cards you collect. On the back write Y, N, or M for Yes, No, Maybe significance. I also write notes on the card or the Post-it so that I do not forget who the people are and what services they provide. I even try to put faces to the cards by writing a brief description. These people will be amazed that you can remember them the next time you meet and they will then want to talk to you.

I then keep my cards in a separate resealable bag for each type of card, for easier follow up. I also make note of the event we attended. This gives me a record of what we were there for and also helps me to keep track of which are the best events for attracting business. If you are starting out cold, then keeping records will be very important—just remember not to collect every card on the floor.

13.Putting It on Paper

Why would you want to write information on paper
when you have a business card in hand?

Putting it on paper can mean a number of things. It can simply mean putting notes on the back of someone's business card, or it can mean taking extensive notes in a notebook. Whichever method you choose, be sure to identify who you were conversing with. Nothing is more embarrassing than talking to a person sometime in the future and finding out you are talking about something she knows nothing about.

If you remember some of Leslie Nielsen's movies, you may remember the one in which he starts talking with a business executive about a project he is starting. He has mistakenly identified this person as the one who hired him. As you can imagine, by the end of the scene, Leslie Nielsen is looking for a place to hide so he can disappear until he finds the correct individual. Name recognition was the difficulty in this case.

Here is another example: a buyer from a company walks in and says he wants to order the usual and then walks out. If the salesperson does not recognize his face or cannot remember his name, that order may never be filled—total embarrassment for the salesperson. The same can happen to you if you do not take the time to write things down on paper. Meticulous notes are not necessary, but if you want to remember, you must put in some key factors that will jog your memory in the future. Practice going back to the person at the same event and repeat her name and go back to one of the points she made.

Also, a lot can be told from the prospects' business cards: are they original, colorful, on good stock, informative, tasteful? Now that you have all the information you want from the other person, you should make sure that she knows about you. You have given your pitch, asked your questions, collected her card, made notes and are ready to take the next step. You need to have something that will catch the prospect's attention and make her remember you. Most often that something is your business card.

14. Your Business Card

What are you trying to say with your business card?

We have talked about collecting other people's business cards and about how they are often tough to differentiate from one another. This is one problem you should avoid for your own business card. It is easier to get into a conversation when you have a business card that speaks for itself. My card, BizMechanix, is so different that almost everyone remarks on how good the card looks. Some people have even said that it is the most professional and great looking card they have ever come across. You should make sure that yours is as impressive. Spend time with a graphic designer, and also take time to buy good paper stock for printing. You are more likely to get notices and gain business if your card is extremely professional.

Do not use the homemade variety—the serrated edges are a sure give-away that you do not value your card. Remember that your card is the first thing people will see on their desk after the event. It is also your card that they will take note of when entering new names into their contact management system. Take the time and make the effort to create something unique, tasteful, and colorful. You do not have to go overboard with it—just make it well worth it. I would rather have an excellent business card than a new car to drive. Most people will not see my car inside the event, but they will see my business card. Do not make it gaudy, just noticeable.

All the pieces have come together and the event has been a success for you. You have made the most of your attendance and practiced the necessary skills. Now it is time to close in on the potential business. The first thing to do is to sort your contacts in order of importance and potential size of the deal. Choose the most important possibility, analyze the potential, and then follow up.

15.Following Up

What happens when you meet a potential client at
an event and you do not follow up?

So now the event is over and you have collected a number of business cards, taken notes on the best prospects, divided the cards into Y(es), N(o), and M(aybe). Now what? It is time to follow up. The best follow-up is immediate—your prospects will remember you best if you go home that night and enter their information into your database and send a personal e-mail or hand-written note. E-mail is of course much faster, and you will be surprised at the fast response you get. This gives you instant contact and you can then ask how they felt about a certain event. You are sure to get a response. This gives you an immediate relationship with the prospect.

Fast response gives you an edge on the competition. You had a reason to follow up—the event—and a further reason—to set a time for that all-important appointment with the right person. You may have talked with this prospect extensively at the meeting and now want to discuss your business relationship further. The ultimate goal of attending an event is to get to the next step: an appointment with certain individuals you feel you would like to do business with.

It is not rocket science that you will have a common goal in business—after all, that is the type of person you sought to be introduced to in the first place. You have a quasi-relationship in the fact that you were both at the same event and in the fact that you followed up promptly. Sometimes the person you are talking to at an event may want to talk again at a later time. Write it down and follow up.

Checklists

Define Your Expertise

What are the things that I love to do in business (list 5)?

_____

_____

_____

_____

_____

What are the things in which I consider myself as an expert?

_____

_____

_____

_____

_____

What do I find easiest to sell?

_____

_____

_____

_____

_____

Define Your Best Customer.

In what areas do I make the most money?

_____

_____

_____

_____

_____

What is the size (measured in people or revenue) of the company that I prefer to sell? Describe in detail.

_____

_____

_____

_____

_____

What industries do I currently sell to?

_____

_____

_____

_____

What industries would I prefer to sell to?

_____

_____

_____

Creating Your Pitch

Why would a customer want to buy from me?

_____

_____

_____

_____

_____

What is my core competency?

_____

_____

_____

_____

_____

List the benefits of buying from me (do not list the features but state what I or my product can do for them).

_____

_____

_____

What is my Pitch?

_____

_____

_____

_____

_____

Which Events to Attend Checklist

Attendees Name	Potential Business

Weekly Event Schedule

Monday:

_____

_____

Tuesday:

_____

_____

Wednesday

_____

_____

Thursday

_____

_____

Friday

_____

_____

Saturday

_____

_____

Sunday

_____

_____

Know the Audience

Name and location of the event I am attending.

_____

_____

_____

_____

Names of attendees that I personally know.

_____

_____

_____

_____

_____

_____

Names of people that I wish to have a personal introduction.

_____

_____

_____

_____

_____

_____

_____

Questions to Ask:

To grab the attention of any potential business client you will need to ask questions that probe for substantive answers rather than a yes or no. Use this list to create your questions for a company that you would like to do business with.

If _____

_____

_____

How_____

_____

_____

Why_____

_____

_____

What_____

_____

_____

When_____

_____

_____

Who_____

_____

_____

Business Card Checklist

Event Attended: _____

Date of the Event: _____

Business Name	Contact Name	Potential & Follow-up date
_____	_____	_____
_____	_____	_____
_____	_____	_____
_____	_____	_____
_____	_____	_____
_____	_____	_____
_____	_____	_____
_____	_____	_____
_____	_____	_____
_____	_____	_____
_____	_____	_____
_____	_____	_____
_____	_____	_____
_____	_____	_____
_____	_____	_____

2. What to Join

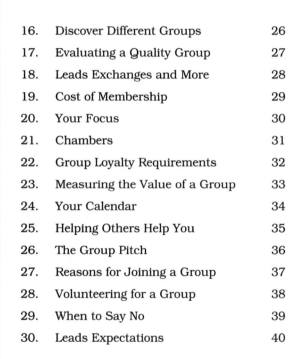

16.   *Discover Different Groups*

What should you look for in a group?

How many business leads groups have you heard about? I have heard of dozens, and each has a membership of 20 or more people. Such groups can be quite useful to you. The problem is that they often restrict the number of people admitted in a particular category, which, fortunately or unfortunately, limits the number of groups that you can choose from. Sometimes a group will have several chapters, especially when one group gets too large and yet still more people in the same category want to join. These splinter groups often start small but then find themselves also straining at the seams.

So how do you find the right group for your business? It pays to research. Let me say it again: It pays to research! I suggest that you get yourself invited to several groups and test the waters. Even if you are in the same category as someone else, you should find a way to be invited. You will not find out how the meetings are conducted and how leads are handled unless you become a participant at one or two of their meetings. Let the group know that you are looking for the perfect group to join and are researching how leads are handled.

You can also find out a lot about a group by contacting not only current but also past members. It is best to include in your survey members who are advocates, some who have left the group for various reasons, and some who are only half-hearted members.

Once you have conducted your research, you can decide which group is best for you. And this is where your business comes in. You will need to take your research one step further and compare what each group targets as its customers with *your* ideal customer.

Another reason for doing the research is that the group also expects *you* to be a customer. For example, a group that is composed of dentists, doctors, and other health professionals will not be ideal for a company selling beauty products. On the other hand, the group would be ideal for cleaning supplies and computer technology.

17. *Evaluating a Quality Group*

When it comes to quality, how do you choose
the group that matches your expectations?

Be picky about the quality of the group you are considering joining;
make sure the group offers what you need. Evaluating the quality of
a group is not as easy as it looks. After you have conducted your
research into meetings, type of attendance, and so on, you will next
want to know the size of the group. Size does count, as a smaller
group will often not have enough leads for each individual unless
they are going after similar customers.

You should also make sure that group members are at the
appropriate level in their companies or businesses. That is, is this
group member someone who *influences* decisions in his company or
is he the person who *makes* the decisions? Often it is the company's
salesperson who attends these group meetings. The salesperson can
often lead you to the decision maker in the company, and often has
leads into other organizations, but this route can be the long way
around to getting business. The decision maker does not necessarily
need to be the CEO, but it is likely to be someone at the
administrative or executive level. Give the pass to groups whose
members do not have direct access to the decision makers;
influencers can have some effect, but in the long run, if they cannot
get you in front of the decision maker, you are most likely wasting
your time.

So, the leads you can potentially obtain through a given group need
to be of some value and they need to include an introduction to the
company needing your services. Let's take a closer look at some of
the types of groups that could possibly fit your needs.

18. Leads Exchanges and More

What is the definition of a leads exchange
and how does it differ from other groups?

So what is a leads exchange? A leads exchange comes in several flavors; first the exchange usually has exclusivity restrictions so that you remain loyal to only one group. This way the printer and the chiropractor who belong to this group will only think of you for a particular service or product. They will essentially promote your business as part of the membership requirement: to generate leads for others as well as get leads in exchange.

These types of groups are plentiful and can work for you or against you. If you have done your homework so you are in a group that is active in the areas in which you would like to be known, this type of group will work well for you. If you work in an unusual business, it may be more difficult for others to find leads for you. Members in this type of group will expect that you have defined your best customer and have given them the tools they need in order to seek out business in that area.

The best way to work this type of group is to generate many leads for others in the group. Once they know you are out to make the most of your end of group membership, they will bend over backward to ensure that you get enough leads so that you will continue to be an outstanding member of the group. They know that if you are dissatisfied, you are likely to look elsewhere and take your great lead generation ability to a rival group. In this environment the more you give, the more you will get.

Leads exchanges provide many opportunities, but there are also some disadvantages to belonging. If you are focusing on your own business, then generating leads for others is a definite detractor. That is, if you are not concentrating on your own leads but instead start concentrating on gaining leads for others, you will find that you are draining away time and effort you would prefer to put into your own business. You might feel at a disadvantage if generating leads for others is your only way to get leads for yourself. You might prefer to go about generating your own leads and uncovering leads that can be fulfilled by another member's business as a by-product. The important thing to remember is that there is always a cost to joining a group.

19.   *Cost of Membership*

When it comes to cost,
how much do you want to spend?

You must weigh several factors before you make your final decision on joining a group. One factor is the cost of membership. When you consider cost, the first thing that likely comes to mind is the monetary costs of membership. Leads groups can cost anywhere from the price of a meal and an extra $20 to a few thousand dollars per year. Although money may be a consideration when looking at costs, you need to make sure that you have enough detailed information on the group to properly analyze what you are getting into.

In addition to financial considerations is the cost of time that you must commit to the group. A weekly two hour meeting in the early evening hours will not likely have much effect on the time you need to generate your own leads for business. However, a commitment to attending weekly group meetings for lunch or dinner may cause your client base to suffer if these meetings conflict with client requirements. On the other hand, the time cost of commitment can be low if fewer meetings are required and they occur at convenient times.

Before you make the commitment, review not only the time it will take to work the group, but also the returns you will get from membership. For example, many groups have guest speakers on topics that are relevant to business and will likely add to the value of your participation. Do not forget to look at membership as part of the investment you need to make in order to improve your bottom line. What will be your return on investment with a given group? It is best to know these factors in advance.

Also learn what criteria are used to remove people from a group. It is one thing to consider yourself a well-accepted member and it is another to be asked to leave. You need to be definitive about your own personal focus.

20. *Your Focus*

Why do you need to know your focus
when joining a group?

The power of focus will differentiate you from the rest of the crowd. You need to concentrate on where business for your organization comes from. Without focus, you will fall into the trap of being the do-it-all person with no particular expertise. In Chapter 1 we talked about making sure you knew your pitch and how you wanted to present yourself to others. Focus has everything to do with how you meet and greet others in all situations. You need to become the specialist for another organization and become ingrained in their activities so that they rely on you for your expertise.

So how do you obtain the focus? You need to take time to really define the direction in which you want your business to grow and how you will get there. It is not about how much business you do or what you do, it is more about how you focus on the services and products your company provides. Focus can be a culmination of things.

First it can be focusing on the business activities you conduct on a daily basis. You may decide to focus on getting ten appointments each month, or perhaps going to three networking events.

Secondly, your focus could be on balancing your work life with your family life. Or perhaps your focus is simply to grow your business.

If you are focused on gaining more business, then it is wise to spend your money and your time in the most appropriate place. Networking and leads groups will help you in this endeavor. Other groups will help you to focus on being recognized for working with other businesses and providing support. If you focus on your business, you can gain respect and make inroads by joining a Chamber of Commerce.

21. *Chambers*

When is the Chamber of Commerce
ideal for your business?

Joining a Chamber of Commerce is likely the best thing any business or individual can do. Chambers provide many benefits to members. They host networking events, usually called business mixers. They also hold local trade shows that draw businesses from other communities, increasing the possibilities of making deals. Chambers are also known for promoting businesses locally through events, Web sites, and tourist bureaus. The cost of membership is not usually large, especially for smaller to medium size companies.

Membership also presents the opportunity to become involved with various committees, sponsoring events, and even becoming a keynote speaker for luncheons or dinners. The Chamber is an excellent way to keep up to date with business issues both locally and county- and statewide. And unlike leads groups, they have no restrictions on the number of members in any category.

They also help you promote your business through newsletters and flyers that are distributed to the business community. You may also have the opportunity to put on a special event for Chamber members, offering them a discount to a program you are hosting. Chambers give you a voice and provide you with a vehicle to promote business ethics within the community.

Chambers are an excellent vehicle for start-ups and small businesses, but they are a voice for medium size businesses as well. Chambers do not have requirements for membership other than keeping your dues current and living up to standard business ethics. Chambers do not have loyalty requirements, and you can join as many Chambers as you wish. This is often advantageous when you do business in several cities. Other groups have strict loyalty requirements.

One last thing to note: your competition may also belong to the Chamber! It is very important to know all you can about your competitor and this is easier through Chamber membership.

22. *Group Loyalty Requirements*

How can you find out the group loyalty
requirements before you venture forth?

Many groups have loyalty requirements in order to make sure that
the leads you generate are exclusively for the members of the group.
Since loyalty requirements can put a damper on other activities you
may have planned, this is yet another detail you need to address
before committing to a given group. If you find a group that has no
requirements for loyalty, you will still have to interview members to
see what other groups they belong to. If there is no focus on your
group, the leads will likely be fewer than you want.

Loyalty requirements that exclude membership in organizations
such as Chamber membership or speaking groups are reason to
strike the group from your list of acceptable groups. Loyalty should
be restricted to other leads groups. Make sure that other members
do buy into the loyalty issue. Often when there is a rule, someone
will take advantage and belong to other groups in a different area.
Loyalty will prove to be the making or breaking of any group.

If you do business with members of other groups, then you should
make sure that they do not have restrictions on whom they may do
business with. Some groups restrict using an outside source for
some services from members. For example, one of the groups I was
considering imposed the condition that joining members were
required to drop their current printer service and give their business
to the member printer. It is NEVER wise to lose good business
relationships through group loyalty requirements.

Loyalty, in theory, is supposed to lead to a closed group that
supports your business and that of the other members. It does not
necessarily mean that you cannot do business outside the group
(you will have to make sure that this is not a requirement). Loyalty is
often only one of the criteria for membership; as you have seen, you
may also have an attendance factor and a fee. In light of the criteria,
you still have to measure the value.

23. *Measuring the Value of a Group*

How do you measure a
group's worth to your organization?

There are several ways that the value of a group can be measured. First, you will need to assess the current membership. Develop a scale of 1 to 10 and give each member a rating based on a set of predefined criteria. What criteria should you use? That will depend entirely on your goals for belonging to the group. For example, if you are selling services for repairing computers, you may rate members by the number of computers they have at the workplace, and you may also add a factor for who they are currently using on the servicing side.

It is best to define at least three criteria for a sampling of the members. You will not want to measure every member; a small cross-section will do. Second, you should measure the amount of business each member (or a sample of members) has received by joining the group. You may also want to know how much business they do with other group members as well.

Once you have the measurements, these same criteria should be applied to each of the other groups you are interested in. Next you will want to do a comparison of the groups and then make your selection based on facts rather than emotion.

Now that you have thought out and used a measurement tool for deciding the value of a group, you will want to test as many groups as possible. You may decide to join only those groups that measure in the top 20% of your scale. One thing you may want to consider is the time and place of the meetings. Your calendar must be open and flexible enough to deal with attendance requirements.

24. *Your Calendar*

When do you want to
make time for a networking group?

One of the most valuable tools you have is your calendar. This tool actually rules how you conduct your day. If you take control of your calendar, you will actually be able to control most of what happens to you at work (and at home). You need to spend a small amount of time each day reviewing your calendar for the next five working days. Yes, you will have appointments beyond five days but the most important ones will be in the next few days. You should always plan your calendar so that it fits your travel and administrative time.

A calendar cannot just be appointments and meetings, you must also schedule when the actual work of putting together a proposal or servicing a customer will take place. The calendar should also include "down time" for you to catch your breath, and don't forget that you need to keep up with the latest business developments in your niche.

A person who is not able to control her calendar will find that each day has a new challenge—how to get everything done in eight hours or less. Quite often this challenge is never conquered unless the calendar is controlled by careful planning. You must plan your networking meetings and also plan to follow up and send out information you have promised. A good calendar will allow you to make better business relationships.

Planning is one of the keys to a successful business. The plan does not have to be elaborate; it simply has to show you what your daily limitations are and also what extra "emergency" time you have built in. For example, some doctors will build in a little slack time for drop-ins or emergencies. They know ahead of time that there is a good chance that there will be a need, and if there is not, then other things will fill the void. Part of your planning should also include time when you can help others, and so maybe you have time to receive help too!

25. *Helping Others Help You*

Why are your focus and pitch
important in any group?

One of the important things to remember is that you can help yourself by being very helpful to others. I remember a person who sent his customers relevant technology articles so that they could keep up with changes in their industries. This person never asked for more business but simply kept in touch by sending out information and tidbits to help others do their work more efficiently. You know the saying, You reap what you sow. This is so true in business. This person formed more solid relationships by constantly giving, and these people he gave to thought of him first when the need to contract someone came up. He eventually got a lot of business in return.

You can also help others help you by simply asking them for advice, or by letting them know what it is you do best. If the other person in the relationship has no idea what you do, how can he or she possibly help you? Using the information reminders scenario, you can also send out information from your field that will help others. For example, if you are an expert in using Excel, send a person who uses it extensively articles or special tips.

One of the best things you can do to help others help you is to sit down with several people for a roundtable discussion. Center the discussion on what you and the others need at the moment. This need does not have to be business related; it could be anything from your need for a plumber, a person to watch your children, or simply a ride to a meeting. Others in these discussions will recommend solutions, and now you have a point of connection with that person that may turn into business in the future.

By helping members of a group, you will gain trust and respect from them. You will find that most people are willing to help you as well. The important thing to remember is that you complete your detailed research of the group and then provide help to substantiate your potential membership. You do not need to push business all the time, but you do need to give something all the time. At the same time, be cognizant of the other members' pitches so that you do not step on toes unnecessarily.

26. *The Group Pitch*

How does the group pitch itself
to you and what is its importance?

Each group has its own definition of how things should be done. Many groups are regimented and require filling out forms and reporting all leads, and other groups take things in a very relaxed manner. Group dynamics have a definite impact on how you do business through the group. Part of your research should entail finding out all the rules in spite of how they pitch their membership.

Several groups in my area of California state that they are the premium group that guarantees you will get more business by becoming a member. What I find is that each group has a set of easy-to-promote businesses. If you are in a business that is not an "easy sell," I would suggest that no matter what the group's pitch, you are not going to get many leads. You will still pay the price of membership and put in the effort of finding work for others, but you may not reap very much in return.

When a group pitch does not give you details of the types of members that are currently in the group, you should be cautious about joining. Make sure you attend as a guest for more than one meeting. The first meeting is often just a dating game; the rules can sometimes change when it turns into a marriage.

If you have any concerns about how a group operates or the type of members it attracts, you should reconsider the need to become a member. If you decide that the group pitch and the results of the research you have done suit what you have in mind, then joining that group may be good for your business. Just make sure that you are clear in your mind and can justify the time and money you will spend on membership.

27. Reasons for Joining a Group

Let's define your purpose for joining a group.

Before you make the decision to join a group, first make sure that you have a clear understanding of what you want to gain from the group. If you are there for business only, make sure that you have as much to give others as you expect to get from the group. Business purposes are genuinely straightforward, and nothing else will get in the way. If, on the other hand, you are there to develop your social skills and gain good relationships with the other members, you should make time to get to know the members first before you join.

Socializing is not usually a big part of leads groups, but you can make it your focus if you choose to. If you want to have lasting relationships built through such organizations, then you should endeavor to provide information, insights, and leads to others in the group. This is the best way to gain their business.

Another great reason for joining a group could be to hone your leadership skills. You can show others that you know how to work with people and therefore would be a good person to do business with. You have to remember that when you are new to a group, others do not know who you are and you have not proven your skills as a product or service provider. If you choose to be a leader in the group, you should take care to provide excellent service first and then become a part of the leadership team.

So why should you become involved? You should look at the three distinctive areas: business only, socialization, and, finally, leadership.

Making the decision on which group to join is not the easiest task, but it will not be the last decision you make. Some groups, such as associations, trade organizations, Chambers of Commerce, have a leadership team and committee that require volunteers. The best way to get to know other members is to volunteer to do something for the group. They will certainly have the opportunity to get to know you better.

28. *Volunteering for a Group*

When is it appropriate to
volunteer to take a position in the group?

Have you heard the saying that "the fastest way to get anything done is to ask a busy person"? It is very true. What it actually boils down to is the fact that busy people are often very well organized and have the ability to delegate some of their tasks. A busy person can usually fit more into her schedule than most people.

For example, I am working a fulltime job which takes at least 55 hours a week, plus I am completing studies for a doctoral degree. That seems like a busy person but that is not all I have on my plate: I also own a company that provides sales process consulting, I volunteer as the Historian for my Rotary District, I make time to exercise twice daily, I tend to my family and write books. On top of all this I still have time to volunteer for committee work at the Chamber of Commerce and spend time with my family. How do I accomplish so much? I organize my day and my week ahead of time and slot everything into its place.

I feel that when you volunteer for an organization, it is your opportunity to give something back instead of always taking; it has its own rewards and it brings in more business. It is an opportunity to lead, support, and nurture a group.

Volunteering also has many other rewards. You become more known in the community, people look to you for your expertise, you become looked on as dependable, you become considered an important person, and people want to know you. Volunteering does take time but so does cold calling. Volunteering will yield much higher results in the long term.

29. *When to Say No*

When is it a good thing to say no to a request?

Balance in one's life is perhaps the most important goal for busy people. They can take on many more projects than most others. They also have the ability to say no if they feel they cannot do a good enough job to satisfy their own criteria. They will often say no if the potential project falls outside their scope of expertise. Saying no does not mean they will not help you find someone else to take on the project. Often busy people know a lot of others who would enjoy becoming involved. Have you ever wished you had not taken on a volunteer position because you find it has become tedious and is taking too much of your time? I am sure all of us have been in that position at one time or another. It often happens that we do not know how to say no, or if we do say no we are not forceful enough to make it understood that we cannot take on the project.

So how do you get around projects that will be too much for you to do, such as becoming the head of a committee that will provide special services to a group? Often you can take on the leadership role and delegate most of the work to the committee members. Although you will still have to devote some time, and you will get recognition, you will only be the leader of the working team. For example, you take on the task of being the head of the social committee and have the committee plan the events and then delegate each event to one of the committee members while you simply oversee.

The important part to remember when volunteering for an organization is to go into it with your eyes open. You cannot expect to be successful with a group if you do not have the time to go the extra mile. Remember that strong business relationships are built over time. It takes a great deal of time to gain credibility and to make inroads within a group, and finally to receive the desired leads from the group.

30.   *Leads Expectations*

How many leads do you pass on?

As a reminder, you must give a lot before you can expect any leads from the group. Not only must you be able to define your best customer, give your pitch, and describe what you do best, on top of this you must gain credibility. After all this, how do you know how many leads to expect? If you have done your homework, you will have a good idea about what you can expect of each member in the group. If the group does an average of one lead per person in the group per week, then you have hit a high note. The biggest problem with getting a lead is the fact that you do not know whether that lead is actually qualified to buy your product or service.

Once you are a long-time member, you can expect to get more leads and better leads. Make sure that your group is one in which the leads you do get come with an introduction. Without the introduction, the lead may as well be a cold call. Sometimes people bring in leads that have potential but with no explicit assurance that the person or company is looking for a particular product or service.

You want to make sure that you do not get anything but qualified leads. To make sure the leads are qualified, you need to let the group know exactly what you are looking for and how you can obtain that business. If you have helped the group help you, then you can expect to receive at least three or four good leads a month.

Do not confuse a lead with a referral. There is a big difference between the two. A lead is something that a second party believes is needed by a third party he or she knows. A referral is what you get when a business is in need of your services and will have a meeting with you to discuss what you can do for them.

Checklists

Group Survey

Name of the group:

_____

Where does the group meet?

_____

Day and time of meetings (is it weekly, bi-monthly, or monthly):

_____

Group Size: _____

How many people do you know in the group? _____

Group Focus: _____

Decision Making Level of the participants:

_____

Are there exclusivity requirements? _____

Number of Leads expected:

Receive in a month: _____ Give in a month: _____

Further Comments:

_____

_____

_____

_____

Membership Assessment Checklist

Name:_____

Criteria (list 3)   Rating (1 to 10)

1. _____   _____

2. _____   _____

3. _____   _____

Potential Business (total)

_____   _____

Name:_____

Criteria (list 3)   Rating (1 to 10)

1. _____   _____

2. _____   _____

3. _____   _____

Potential Business (total)

_____   _____

Name:_____

Criteria (list 3)   Rating (1 to 10)

1. _____   _____

2. _____   _____

3. _____   _____

Potential Business (total)

_____   _____

Daily Calendar:

Time Slot	Activity
_____	_____
_____	_____
_____	_____
_____	_____
_____	_____
_____	_____
_____	_____
_____	_____
_____	_____
_____	_____
_____	_____
_____	_____
_____	_____
_____	_____
_____	_____
_____	_____
_____	_____
_____	_____

NOTES

3. Strategic Alliances

31. *Why Form Alliances*

What is the biggest advantage of forming an alliance?

Why an alliance? An alliance is another way to do business without having to use your own sales force. Alliances give you the advantage of enabling you to offer more products and services that are related to your core business. Everyone has his or her own definition of an alliance, and here is one of my experiences that will help you put you own definition together.

I had a potential alliance with a person who was starting his own business. He came to my residence with his partner and I brought in a couple of friends and business associates to discuss the possibilities. He gave us a fabulous demonstration of his company offerings. I really liked what he had to offer and was willing to pass leads on to him. He was excited about the possibilities. He next mentioned that he would love to work with our current client base. I asked how he saw the relationship working and his reply was that he would piggyback on our current sales effort. I then asked him how we could capitalize on his client base and how he would help sell our services.

Guess what. He only wanted a one-way relationship: we would make money on sales we did for him! This would certainly divert from our core business, taking us into another area which might fit within our focus in some respects, but not entirely. Needless to say, this potential alliance did not get put on paper, even though his offerings were good. You see, an alliance has to be a two-way street. Each member must derive a benefit from forming it.

In this example, the business presented would not be a good choice for an alliance. We needed to have a company that provided us with services we could offer in addition to our own services. The allied company would also have the opportunity to sell our services as an add-on. The important thing to remember is that you must choose your alliances carefully. Any alliance should take into consideration how to guarantee business from both parties.

32. *Who Makes the Best Alliances*

What types of companies
do you want to align yourself with?

What is the best company to align with? It is a company that does not quite compete with your core business. That is, the company has offerings that dovetail with what you have to offer. If you were selling tire rims, you would likely want to form an alliance with a company that sells tires. The relationship would work for both companies. Even though you are in the same industry, you each have a different focus. By forming an alliance, you both win.

So how do you find such companies? First, you need to determine what your core business is, and second, what other business would be beneficial for you to offer without taking away from your core. Once you discover the type of business you want to align with, you must do research to see whether prospective candidates for an alliance already have such alliances with your competition. Do not pick just any company and go from there; do your research first. When you think about it, few alliances ever work well that are not based on research.

Some companies are not interested in alliances because they want to have an open field for selling other components that dovetail into their business. When you find a good potential alliance, make sure you approach them with well-researched facts. You must be able to show how an alliance will benefit them as well as you.

Alliances are like partnerships: both parties need to have everything in writing, including statements of expectations. There also must be trust on both sides before an agreement is entered into. It is likely you will call this type of relationship a channel partner, or dealer. Even though these names seem familiar, each type has its own unique expectations. In reality what you are looking for is a good channel partner that will promote your products and services.

Channel partners have many products they resell and if you can find a good partner, you will be able to increase your sales. When looking for an alliance with another company, you should make sure you look in the right places.

33. *How to Find Good Alliances*

Where do you look for the appropriate alliance?

One of the most asked questions is, "How do you find a good alliance partner?" It is actually fairly easy. You can find potential alliances by taking some time to do research. Remember to start by focusing more on finding the potential partner than on implementing the alliance.

Potential alliances can be found by looking at your competition. If the competition is selling to a potential alliance, then so should you. You should also rely on your own business relationships and referrals from your current customer base or contacts. The best possible linkages are obtained through referrals. Yes, there are other ways to get potential partners and those can also be explored—but they take a little longer to cultivate. We will look at other methods later in this chapter.

The first step in your careful planning is to draft a list of possible candidates. You next need an affirmative answer to each of the following questions: Is there a demand for your products or services in the potential partner's market? Is the potential partner open to adding your products or services to its current line of business? Is there likely sufficient profit for the alliance to work?

Once you have identified potential alliances, make sure you gather enough information about what they do, what they sell, and how they conduct business with their customers. You will need to be armed with plenty of information about them and how your products and services fit into their catalog.

You must also find a place to put the products and services being offered by the alliance. If you have done your homework, trading catalog entries should not be a problem. You want to form an alliance only where you both benefit from the connection.

34. How to Make the Approach

When you find a good match, what happens next?

When you locate the ideal alliance partner and you are ready to start talks, you may want to set up roundtable discussions with the potential partner. Prepare by listing what you want the contract to contain and go through the agreement with the potential partner so that both parties are satisfied with the end result. One thing to remember before you even walk in the door or any contract is in place is that the result should always be a win-win. Once contract negotiations are done, you should not feel that you have given away the farm, nor should you feel that you have taken most of the value out of the agreement.

You also want to make certain that the potential partners have acted ethically in all their business dealings, and also that their customers are more than just satisfied. Where do you get this information? Your first source is the potential partner. For the interviews, prepare a series of questions that enable you to assess the partner's integrity and the customer service it currently offers to all types of its customers. You will have some idea of how well its business is received.

You need to add performance expectations into the agreement as well, which includes their sales expectations and your marketing efforts on their behalf, and vice versa. Remember, this is an alliance, and initially you will both have an expectation of an increase in business—increased sales and profits—for both parties. Nothing is worse than having someone set up to sell your products and nothing happens.

In order to make sure that sales happen on the partner's side, you will need to provide training on how to sell your products and also marketing and sales tools in the form of demo CDs, brochures, and other printed materials. The provision of such materials and services should be a part of the agreement. It may seem like a one-sided burden at the beginning, but you will have a lot to gain in the long run. Letting everyone know about the new alliance and networking with the partner's customers will ensure that the alliance is successful.

35. *What do you Gain?*

How can you measure the
potential gains from an alliance?

To measure your potential gain from an alliance, the first thing you will need to look at is the return on your investment in the partner. If you invest time and money in the partnership, when will you be able to reap a profit or at least break even? In my estimation, you should give one fiscal quarter to learning your products and services with minimal sales, but in the second quarter you should expect a marked improvement and a break-even and minimal profit. Not all alliances will be so slow off the mark, since they may have previous experience in the product line. You may find that some alliances are instantly profitable, although on average you should expect profits at a minimum of two quarters down the road.

Remember that the main thing you are interested in is the relationship you will build with the alliance partner. This relationship will lead to the introduction of other customers that they are working with. The expanded network that you will nurture is of prime importance, and the profits should be looked at as a side benefit of the relationship. We all enter into agreements in the hopes of making money; a good business relationship will usually bring in the profits you expect. But the support and nurturing of the relationship is what will bolster the sales in the long run. Profits will be multiplied if you work on keeping your relationship alive, and you must be able to provide service above and beyond expectations.

Let us recap the potential gains if everything goes well.

You will have:

- ✓   a partner that is willing to sell your products or services.

- ✓   a solid business relationship that you can rely on for advice and improvement.

- ✓   a partner that will aid you in the increase of your bottom line.

To make sure you keep the alliance alive, you will need to focus on how you can nurture it and make it grow.

36.   *How to Nurture the Relationship*

What are the best methods for
maintaining a good business relationship?

Once you have a business relationship in place, you need to work on it to keep it intact. As a matter of fact, many people nurture their business relationships more than they do their own families! The first and most obvious method is to answer questions and fulfill requests in a timely manner. This rapid response to queries does more for the relationship than sending out regular information. Customers or business partners are really impressed with response rates.

Can you imagine being in a retail store and asking the sales clerk a question about the product you are about to purchase and he says he will get back to you in a minute but actually finishes a phone call, chats with a few others in the store, and then starts another project before getting around to the answer? It is likely you would walk out on such a situation. The same is true when forming solid relationships with customers and partners. The sooner you respond, the more likely are they to want to do business with you.

Likewise, the partner will need to nurture the relationship. Relationships are two-way streets. You cannot always give the information and solve all the problems; there must be something in return for you. Usually this is in the form of sales or introduction to other potential business relationships.

There is a fine line between nurturing a business relationship and making clear what is in it for the partner. The difference is often difficult to discern, but when you discover where it lies, the business relationship will grow even further.

37.   *What's in It for Them*

How do you make sure your
alliance partner is satisfied?

Do not forget that a partner or alliance is only interested in what is in it for them. They may see you as a cash cow or they may see you as an opportunity to further their current business. Whatever their perspective on the alliance, they will likely want to make sure that they have a real winner on their side. This doesn't mean that you have to lose; it simply means that you have to be aware of what motivates them into becoming an alliance partner. You will also need to be aware that they will not be motivated to help you in your business unless you are motivated to help them in theirs.

As an example, I once had a small Internet-based company as a client. They wanted to set up alliances on the Web so that others would also sell their products. The idea was great and we proceeded to set up others to sell for them. But the company ran into a problem: the additional sales were minimal.

The reason was simple: once the alliance was set up, the company ignored the needs of the alliance partners; all they expected were results. As you can imagine, there was no motivation for the alliance to make the sale. One other problem also occurred with this setup: the alliance partners were not screened so as to identify what their focus in the marketplace was. The company simply wanted to have their products sold in as many places as possible.

Although the premise for the alliance was good, there was little satisfaction for the reseller other than just potential profit. The lines of communication were minimal at the most, and the only tracking that occurred was to gauge how many sales were made. There were no specific milestones that were mutually beneficial and therefore the problem of minimal sales became exponential. There was no opportunity to leverage the new relationship.

38. *Why Leverage*

Why should you leverage the relationship?

Leveraging sometimes carries negative connotations—leveraged buyouts with their junk bonds, leveraged portfolios with risky assets and borrowed funds. Leveraging does not have to be thought of that way, or as a way for one business to step on another business to make its own headway. Leverage is also simply power or effectiveness. Leveraging within alliances can make both parties more profitable and solidify their business relationship. If you work with the alliance partner, you will both be able to leverage the relationship for mutual benefit.

For example, a store I once worked with wanted to leverage its relationship with its several channel partners. A meeting was set up with one partner to discuss how the relationship could be expanded to benefit both parties. It was discovered that the partner wanted to learn more about the products the company was selling and get more involved in training its customer base. The parent company on the other hand wanted to find ways to support the customers of the partner in order for the partner to gain more sales.

In this case, both parties were able to leverage the other's contacts and offer better customer service. The channel partners also were able to find additional customers because they had more of an inside track on the products being offered. They were able to train new customers and give a new dimension to their offerings. The parent company profited from the additional sales, as did the partner.

Through leveraging the current customer base and the product lines, both companies could offer better customer service. As a result of this success, the parent company offered the same alternatives to other channel partners and found that most of them welcomed the additional opportunity.

To be successful, the opportunity has to be presented to the right level of decision makers with an emphasis on potential increase in profits.

39. *Forming the Relationship*

At what level should the relationship be established?

A question that is often asked is "How do you get to the right person in an organization for making the decision?" The answer is not an easy one as some organizations have decision makers at various levels, and of course it depends on the size of the organization. If you are dealing with 10 or fewer employees, you are likely to need to work with the owner or CEO of the organization. It is imperative that you not waste your time dealing with those who cannot make the appropriate decision. If you find that you are dealing with influencers, you know that in the long run they cannot make the decision to go or not to go with the alliance.

So how do you get to the right person? There are many ways, but the simplest way is to start at the top. I know that many CEOs do not want to deal with sales people and certainly not with a lot of the everyday information that comes their way. So getting to them may be a bit difficult. The best way to form a relationship is to appeal to their business pain (that which concerns them the most) and offer a solution to that pain. For example, a company wanted to set up a channel or partner network to sell their products. Since they only had a couple of dealers at the time they were ready to move to the next level. To make the program successful, meetings with company owners had to take place. These owners were offered additional profits as part of the deal. This offering was put in place to ensure the companies would buy into the program.

Profit is not the only way to get to the CEO. You also need to understand her business goals and see how you can fit into the formula before making the approach. The key here is to show that you have something to offer that is of value to the company. The value should not be presented in the form of features of your product or service but a list of benefits.

40. *Alliance Requirements*

How do you make sure you have the
business solutions or services
that your alliance partner needs?

You can only make sure that what you have to offer a company fits
into their goals and mission if you do your research on what drives
that business. If you go in "cold" you are not likely to win any
business as you do not know enough about the company and they
certainly do not know enough about you. You should try and make
your visit from a referral, if at all possible. Learn more about what
solutions they are looking for and get introduced to a few of the key
people in the organization. A business relationship needs time in
order to solidify. If you do not know enough about the inner
workings of the company, you will not likely be able to form an
alliance with that organization.

You must be able to learn about their business pain in order to find
the solution, or a solution, to help them along the path. You may
also have to offer some free advice or service in order to ingratiate
yourself into their business and learn more about their business
model. Once you have gained trust (and you *should* be trustworthy),
it will be much easier to form an alliance that benefits both parties.
The important thing to remember is that you need to get to know the
other company first and then work a solution into the relationship.

Research is one key to making sure you have the appropriate
solution. Other considerations are to conduct an assessment of the
company's customers. We talked about assessments earlier in the
chapter, and I want to emphasize that you will find out more about a
company through assessments than you will through talking to
employees of that firm. Once you have your results, you can take an
integrated approach on how the two companies can form an alliance.
You will be able to weave the fabric of a good business relationship.

41. *When to Monitor an Alliance*

> How do you know when an alliance
> needs to be monitored and tracked?

More often than not, an alliance needs to be monitored and tracked. If you ignore your alliance partner, you will be losing ground and your business relationship will not be what you expect. You know it is a general truth that if you ignore anyone, he tends to forget about you, or at least he will not take you seriously and will find other people to pass the time with. The same is true for an alliance partnership. You should remember to treat your partner just like a customer and always keep in touch. Any business relationship depends on how much you keep in touch and how much information you give your partners to keep the project alive.

This does not mean that you have to commit to a great volume of communications, but you do have to commit to a regular communication strategy, and it has to be a two-way commitment. You must also know what is happening with the alliance partner and how you can help to increase the amount of business she does on your behalf. Two-way commitment and communication should be part of any alliance or partnership agreement you put in place. If you do not make such a commitment, the dialog or information will be sporadic and you will not receive consistent updates on the latest and greatest information. And it is only with information that you will be able to take full advantage of the alliance.

When you spend time monitoring and tracking an alliance, you will be fully prepared to step in with help when it is needed. You will also be advised well in advance of any potential problems. Problems with an alliance can be many, but clear and consistent communication can keep them to a minimum and perhaps even solve them before they become too large and threaten the relationship.

42. When Alliances Are a Problem

How do you determine
potential problems with an alliance?

Alliances and partnerships will always have problems. Nothing ever goes as smoothly as it should. In other words, nothing is easy. The alliance must be nurtured and any possible problem dealt with before it ruins the relationship. So what can go wrong with an alliance?

First, the alliance partner may not be focusing enough on doing well with your product or service. They may want to sell more of another company's products before they deal with yours. You can solve this problem by keeping them informed and educated about what benefits they get out of the alliance with you.

Second, an alliance partner may not gain enough sales of your product or service to be motivated to retain the partnership. You have a choice as to whether to drop and replace them or to work with them to increase sales. If at all possible, you should try to speak the same language. This will earn you more respect in the long run and potentially increase sales.

If you think about it, it is less costly to increase training and support for a current alliance partner than to try and find a new partner. Lastly, an alliance may have changes in personnel, and the new people may not believe in your product line (they may want to sell a competitor's line as their favorite). In this case, the business relationship will need to be rescued through additional communication efforts.

Any number of other problems may arise within an alliance, but the three mentioned are the most common to the partnerships I have created for my company. I often do surveys of my channel partners to judge any lapses of interest. I also look at the number of product returns from any partner because these usually indicate product substitution for another line and thus also indicate a change in focus. You will need to determine your own minimum standards for an alliance and draw that line in the sand as the starting point.

43. *Drawing the Line*

How far can you go in your
relationship with an alliance partner?

The imaginary line you draw in the sand will let you know when an alliance is getting close to failing. I would suggest setting the line a little short of the disaster point. As a matter of fact, the line should sit around 75% of the distance between the ideal and dissolution. This way you can work with the partner before the relationship has sunk too low. Lulls in partners' sales may be a fairly normal occurrence, but when the lulls are compounded by lack of communication and lack of marketing, you know that something else is the underlying problem.

Alliances and partnerships will always have lulls and marketing efforts will sometimes be lax. If you take the time to monitor all the details and be consistent with your support, an alliance partner will not feel that you have overcommitted with other partners to their detriment, and they will still feel that they are important. You should also remember that having a service level agreement in place to define sales, marketing efforts, and first rights of refusal will add to a successful alliance. You must remember that you are the expert in the field and that they will rely on you for help and support.

A word of caution: when it comes to support you should always

✓   support the customers of an alliance partner.

✓   monitor the amount of support you give to each of your
    alliance partners.

✓   educate partners that need more help than others.

You always need a number of touch points in order to be aware of a potential failure. If you do not stay in contact, you risk losing future sales.

44. *Preventing Failure*

When do you know an alliance is falling apart?

An alliance will surely fail without good communication on both sides. It will also fail if the alliance partner is not capable of completing the tasks set out in the service level agreement. Service level agreements are usually put in place so that milestones in the process can be monitored. The agreement also helps to minimize not only the number of complaints by the alliance partner but also the complaints from the partner's customers about the service being provided. Of course, any expectations about the partner's performance assume the basic premise that the products and services being offered are of excellent quality. If the quality is missing in the formula, your alliances will most definitely fail.

Finger pointing is one of the worst things that can happen in a relationship. The old saying goes "never burn a bridge as you never know when you need to cross it again." If you learn to navigate all the major problems through negotiation or better understanding, you will be able to keep the alliance moving forward.

If you let problems stand in the way, you will lose more than just an alliance. Your customers will take sides and sales will plummet. Customers rarely come back once they have been sandwiched between two companies in conflict. To prevent this from happening, try and be aware of things that have begun to go in the wrong direction so that you can solve any problem before it gets out of hand.

Alliances also fail because the return on investment was not as promised. Relationships can be very fickle when it comes to money transactions. You need to build the relationship first, keep it intact, and then deal with the ROI. If the product or service does not live up to expectation, then a mutually agreeable term in the service level agreement should give a way out to one or both parties. This will allow for an amicable departure and keep the personal relationship intact even though the businesses are no long part of an alliance.

45. Capitalize on Existing Alliances

How do you capitalize on existing alliances?

As we mentioned before, it is easier to work with an existing partner and keep that relationship alive than it is to find a new alliance partner. You must make sure that there are plenty of WIFMs (What's in it for me) to keep them happy. An alliance partner will not likely want to continue if they perceive there is not much for them to keep the relationship going. One company I did a contract for always stated that they wanted to "thrill the customer every day." This policy kept their customers coming back for more. And they did not do it by underpromising and overdelivering; it is simply that the work they did was of excellent quality and met or exceeded their customers' expectations.

The word overdeliver gets overused. It has the connotation that someone makes a promise of a milestone that is easy to reach and then does more than expected. Customers get tired of being set up for "overachievement." It is best to set the bar high and then meet that expectation with extreme quality rather than exceeding a lower mark. If you can exceed the mark with great quality then you are not likely setting the bar high enough.

You can only capitalize on existing alliances if you are willing to keep them coming back for more. It is the quality and commitment to their success that will allow the business relationship to thrive. Then and only then will they recommend you to other businesses.

Checklists

Potential Alliance Partners:

Company Name   Benefits

_____   _____

_____   _____

_____   _____

_____   _____

_____   _____

_____   _____

_____   _____

_____   _____

_____   _____

_____   _____

_____   _____

_____   _____

_____   _____

_____   _____

Alliance Analysis:

Name of potential alliance partner:

_____

_____

_____

What I will sell through their company:

_____

_____

_____

What I want from the alliance:

_____

_____

_____

What they want from the alliance:

_____

_____

_____

Will this alliance work? Why or why not?

_____

_____

_____

4. Announcements

46.   *Want Business? Throw a Seminar*

Why is throwing a seminar good for business?

If you want to clean your house, throw a garage sale. If you want to increase business, throw a seminar. A seminar is a way for you to contact many people all at once. It will pull in an audience that is interested in what you have to say. When you put on a seminar, begin by acquiring a mailing list from organizations with potential buyers and add it to your past and present customers. The seminar will draw interest from the subject matter you are presenting. If you have a difficult time attracting attendees, perhaps you need to take another look at your topic. No one will attend a seminar that does not have some impact on his or her business.

The mailing lists you choose to promote the seminar are also important. I recently put on a seminar called "The Seven Deadly Sins of Selling." I was new to the area and was not sure what kind of draw I would get. I had five weeks to get an audience. The first thing I did was to make sure I provided food in the way of a continental breakfast. Next, I sent the invitation to the members of two Chambers of Commerce, my Rotary Club, and other Rotarians with whom I was acquainted. I also asked people I knew if they had suggestions for inviting people they knew; in total I invited 400 people and got 117 reservations. The attendance at the event was 87. I was very pleased.

Through the seminar, I was able to launch my consulting business in the area of "Sales Process Consulting." The leads I obtained through feedback forms were all qualified leads, and when I called them they were all receptive to setting up a meeting with me.

47.   *New Products*

How can the introduction of new products
affect the way I network at meetings?

When I have a new product to launch, I make sure that I have a 20-
to 30-second pitch ready for the next networking event I attend. I
also make sure that I have a supply of product announcements
offering a free sample. As I work through the crowd, I make sure that
I am talking to people who could use my product by listening
carefully to what they have to say, and if the product does not fit I go
on to the next conversation.

The important thing to remember is that you should not force your
product on everyone you talk to. You have a job to listen intently to
what they have to say and then make a judgment as to the fit of
what you have to offer. Sales of new products are not made or
broken through networking events, the products are simply being
introduced so that the next time an event occurs and you have
product to display, some attendees will be aware of your offering. The
important thing is to make sure that you are excited about your
product or service, that you are an expert in the field, and that you
are able to deliver what is promised. All three conditions need to be
present while you are attending an event and making the product
introduction. If one item is missing, the product is not likely to be
well accepted.

Sometimes a networking event will allow participants to have a
display booth. In that case, you should make sure that you have a
table, or share one, where you offer tests or trial sizes with feedback
forms. It is one thing to give out the product; it is another thing to
get feedback on its application. Never give out any product without
having a way to contact the potential user.

48.   *Trial Runs*

Why is a network meeting the best
place to get participants for a trial run?

We talked above about taking a booth at a networking event, or at least sharing a booth or table. The booth has to be more than informational in order to help you move your product or service. I have been to many networking events and have walked by hundreds of booths trying to figure out if what they offer applies to me as a business or as a consumer. The most common thing I see is a table with information, a place to put a business card for a draw (collecting their own mailing list), and a series of brochures that I will likely toss when I get home. It is how you get around the typical table at an event that is important.

First, most people sit behind the table and offer information. They barely move until you go to take some information and then they pounce all over you. If you want to attract more attention to what you are doing, you must move from behind the table and be extremely interactive with those taking a glance at your wares.

Second, at most booths the participants must take the information from the table without much explanation. It is better to have something that is interactive so that the event goer is actually a real participant in your offering. This method will certainly gain their interest in a different way.

Once you have the attention of networking event attendees, you will find more people will want to know what is going on. You have now motivated the audience to sign up for a trial run and you are able to give them a memory that will last.

49.   *Newspaper Relationships*

How do you establish a good relationship with a newspaper so that you can get new contacts?

Newspaper relationships are probably the most difficult relationships to form. Often a newspaper will have different departments that look after advertising, human interest stories, editorials, and daily news. Knowing a person in one department does not necessarily get you credibility in another department. I once had a client who needed to have a good relationship with the local newspaper because he wanted to launch a new product that would have an impact on the labor force. Although the client had been an advertiser in the paper for years, he was having difficulty gaining entry into the other departments of the newspaper. As it turned out, he was not really involved in the community and the paper was only interested in stories about companies that had community involvement.

My client joined two organizations that were held in high regard in the community. He joined the groups that he knew reporters and other newspaper personnel also belonged to. Once he became involved, he got to know these people and soon had no problem getting press releases read. Without the personal contact and some common interest, newspaper relationships are not likely to happen.

Newspaper stories are good for getting your name known in the community. In most areas, people do read the local press. Someone who reads an article about you may give you some recognition and will certainly know where you work. Besides newspaper stories, there are many other ways you can use the media. You can be creative with how you make announcements of new contracts, changes in personnel, or the launching of a new product.

50.   *Press Releases*

How do press releases or interest stories
have an effect on meeting new potential clients?

Press releases can make the difference between being known and being just the same old service that everyone offers. You need to set yourself apart from all your competition. The press needs stories about what is happening in your product or service area. After all, the press has to write stories—why not all about you? But they are not looking for the commonplace activities you provide; they are looking for what is unique about you. You have to determine what they are looking for by reading the newspaper and by learning what the editor or producer is looking for.

You will need to write your press releases to their attention. The press release should always be short—usually only three paragraphs. Present the most important information first, such as your name, credentials, expertise, and your company name. The first paragraph should contain all the exciting things you want to announce.

The remaining two paragraphs should give a little more detail but not too much. You want them to write about you and what you are doing. Some newspapers will want to have other information and you will need to provide a press kit for their reading. Just remember that you should send out a press kit only if the publication requests it or states ahead of time that you need to submit one. A press kit should contain the press release, previously published news, reviews, articles, and other items that prove you are worth the ink. In any case, remember, it is YOU who needs to make the news!

A press release is one way to make an announcement, but there are many other places in the media where you can highlight a company. Newspapers will publish letters to the editor, list your events on their calendar of events, accept suitable articles for publication, and partner with you for community-related causes. Announcements can be placed in many places besides newspapers. Remember, an announcement can be anything that is newsworthy, not just a promotion.

51.   *Happy Announcements*

> When do you use the newspaper for
> publishing announcements for
> promotions or new partnerships?

An announcement in a newspaper will only bring further recognition to your business. Always send items such as the hiring of a new employee, the announcement of a new contract, a change of location, or any other item of information that you would like the world to know. Announcements are a way for you to communicate to the rest of the business community that you are a company on the move. Calendars, business sections, and special sections are some of the choice locations where you can place announcements. You must find the right locations to place your announcements, so you should have a list of the local, regional, and national media that have calendars of events or sections for placing such announcements.

You do not have to put your ego into the announcement; simply stick to the facts so that your potential and existing customers are aware of what you are doing. If they see you making regular announcements, they will perceive you as a company that is on the go. Announcements do not cost anything but time to put together, and time is also what you will need to make sure these announcements get to the right location.

There is no point in doing a media blast to places that would not normally print such items. If you spend too much time annoying such outlets with things they are not interested in, they will recognize your company name, and come the day you have something they should ordinarily be interested in, it is too late; they are likely to disregard it. Nevertheless, the point is that you need to make announcements *all the time*, and you do need to target where these announcements go.

Announcements that get your face in the paper or other media are a good first step, but there are many other ways in which you can take advantage of the press. Newspapers are always looking for items of interest. Turn your announcements into a real interest story and make it unique to you and your business.

52.   *Interest Stories*

What makes a good interest story?

An interest story is just that—an interesting story. It means that you have something interesting to say and therefore have something of interest to be printed. The problem is that everyone else has something of interest to say. You must make your interest story truly unique and something that readers will want to read. Without a twist, you have just a commonplace story that will likely end up in the wastebasket. So how do you make your story interesting?

First, see what the media need. Each newspaper, magazine, or other publication has a different slant to make it more saleable. You will need to gear your story to satisfy the particular needs of each target outlet.

Second, take a close look at your story to make sure it is one that you can repeat quite easily. Do not make things up, because you may find yourself in a position where you are required to defend or expand on the story and will not know what to say.

Last, the story needs to be about a part of how you have defined yourself and your business. It should convey the essence of the company with you as a part of that company. The thrust of the interesting story may be a unique way you have dealt with customers to make them happy, or it may be a technology you invented to fill some unique niche. You must make your story worthy of reading and worthy of printing in the media. An interesting story can be about anything from the way you present your proposals to how you aid other businesses to succeed.

An interesting story is likely to lead some people to contact you immediately, and perhaps other newspapers or publications will also want to know more. You must prepare yourself for writing or being the subject of additional articles and for expanding your story. You will also find that people on the street or at networking events will want to know more too. What a perfect opportunity to pass out your business card.

53.   *Gaining Contacts*

How do you use business
cards to gain new contacts?

Have you ever been to a networking meeting where people are
furiously trading business cards? I most certainly have. It is
sometimes quite frantic. I like to go to all kinds of networking events
in order to have people see my face and to let them recognize who I
am. I find that they want my business card but not for the reasons I
want them to have it. They want to pitch me instead of the other way
around. If you find yourself in this situation, trade the cards but find
out more about the other person and make sure she knows who you
are and how you can help her. You should also make sure that you
write on the back of her card the pertinent information about her.
You need to know what her business pain is, and make notes as to
how you can help her. You can also determine whether she can help
you.

Remember you are also collecting business cards and you are
expanding your database of contacts. You will be able to send your
announcements and other items to these people because you will
have put them on your list. Just remember that you must first ask
them if they want to be on the list. You will find that personal
contact and exchanging cards will almost always result in agreement
to being added to your list. Having a great contact list in any area is
important as long as you remember who they are, where you met
them, and what their business pain really is.

A business card is your front door to another's business. It is your
announcement card. It should be well designed, colorful, with a logo
and only the important contact information. This is not the place to
make an announcement or advertise all your services. It is a place
where you are introduced. In Japan the exchanging of cards is
almost a ceremony and is not taken lightly; you should do the same.
You never know whom you will meet, and your card should be
printed, not homemade, as it reflects your own professionalism!
People will ask you to be more involved if they think you are the right
fit and you have a polished image; no one wants to be sponsored by
a slob.

54. *Sponsorships*

> How do you sponsor an event and get
> personal introductions at the same time?

How can sponsoring help make you visible to the business community and gain the right contacts? It is quite simple: find events that attract the audience in which you are interested. These facts will help you form important business relationships. Find out the following:

- ✓ Whom you wish to do business with

- ✓ Which sports they like

- ✓ What community events they like

- ✓ Where the upper management families live and their community involvement

The events they watch are the ones that you should sponsor. For example, if you want to target the business community in Pleasanton and you find that most of the executives belong to the Rotary Club, and that the club has a number of community events for which they are always looking for sponsors, then take the initiative to either join the Rotary Club (you need to be invited by a member) or find out how you can offer a sponsoring role.

Once you offer the sponsorship, you may find that members of the club are more open to talking with you and helping to support your business in the community. All service and community organizations are looking for sponsors—you just have to find the ones that give you the visibility that you need in the community. You want the business leaders to be aware of your involvement, and also be aware that you are open to their fundraisers for good causes.

Whether you want to believe it or not, money does talk, as long as the money is used appropriately. You should not sponsor things that you do not believe in! Only sponsor and help others where you have the same philosophy and the same interests. Nothing is worse than sponsoring only for the glory and not for the belief in what the organization does. Organizations are also looking for straight donations.

A checklist at the end of this chapter will help you plan for sponsoring an event.

55.   *Donations*

How is a donation different from a sponsorship
and what is the advantage to you?

Donations are different from sponsorships, as a sponsorship is more likely to headline you for an event whereas a donation will let you be listed as one of the many donors. You do not need to headline every event to get business attention; you can simply donate an amount of funds and be listed. You may find that donors are listed in categories of the amount donated. The donations may be cash or they may be in kind.

For example a service club is putting on a fundraiser and needs donations of items for a silent auction and also needs cash donations to offset the cost of the event. You will then be able to decide which is the better option for you and your company. Cash is always welcomed but the item you donate may bring more attention. If an item is unique *and* in demand, it will have bidders warring to purchase it during the auction.

You can donate a major item that will go to a live auction or you may have it be a silent auction item that people read about and see on the tables. You may also donate a door prize that catches attention. I know a person who always donates items to charity events and she is very well known in the community for her involvement and the donations she makes. She sells small makeup related items, and everyone knows what she does and the products she sells. When you are looking for such items, you will likely call her, so donations do work!

When you approach a business that is involved in the community event you donated to, you will have a common bond with that business. You will then have an opening topic of conversation that can lead to better business relationships. You will also have a list of people you can contact for help in your business.

A checklist at the end of this chapter will guide you through the donation process.

56.   *Ask for Help*

Why ask others for help,
and what do you gain from it?

What does asking for help have to do with creating business relationships and making announcements? Everything. You have made announcements, donated items, created an awareness of who you are and what you do. You are now in the position of getting more business than you can handle, or worse, not getting enough business in the community. You should then be able to call on prospective customers and ask for their time to help you solve a particular problem.

The problem must be one that they will be able to help you solve before you ask for their time. For example, you could call a business and ask if they could help you answer some questions about handling a situation you have and that you know they have handled well in the past. You will almost always get a yes to setting the meeting.

Never hesitate to ask others for advice or help on something you say they do well. The person you talk to is impressed and his ego is stroked. This is a good basis for forming a great business relationship. Avoid the negative side, however: Never come across as being too needy. The needier you seem, the more it will turn off the relationship. You will also find that there are a number of groups in your community that support businesses, such as The Executive Council (TEC) or the Alliance of CEOs; you should look into other ways to solve problems and gain contacts at the same time.

Gaining an outsider's insights will also give you a leg up when you are being sought out as a business partner for a project. If you have a give-and-take rapport with your business relationships, you will have a great foundation for being accepted, and also for being recommended to others. You are, after all, in a big race to win the business.

57. *The Big Race*

What is the big race all about
when it comes to creating relationships?

The big race is simply the ability to win the deal consistently. You will need to perfect your message, be able to state it clearly and precisely, and follow up relentlessly. Without all these factors, you are losing ground to the competition. You need to stay ahead at all times by keeping an eye on what your competitors are doing well and not so well. This is your opportunity to capitalize on the competitors' weaknesses and keep up with their strengths. It is not that you have to beat them at their best, but it is important that you at least stay even with their best. What you must do, however, to stay ahead is to do much better at what they do not do well.

In other words, when running the big race, make sure you have a more interesting story, and find out what the competitor is saying and capitalize on its weaknesses and stay on top of its strengths. The race is a win-or-lose competition, the scales are tipped one way or the other by a consistent strategy, and a strategy that emphasizes you but does not bash the competition.

My dad is better than your dad will not work in this economy. Remember that you will always have lots of competition; it is you who must strategize on how to win the race at almost, if not every, turn in the road. You must wear better running shoes to take advantage of outperforming the competition. Capitalize on your strengths and downplay your weaknesses.

The big race is not won without a good attitude. Your attitude toward your customers will either make you or break you at any time in the race. You need to also remind your customers that you are a contender and not a long shot. You must keep them informed at all times. One easy way to keep in touch is through postcards.

58.   *Postcards*

The latest craze is to send a postcard advertisement to everyone on a mailing list. It is both good and annoying to customers. Junk mail, as many call it, does not always get read, but if you put a twist on what is on your postcard, then you are likely to be noticed. A postcard will not yield much business, but in reality it only takes one good contract to pay for the whole mailing.

So how do you use postcards effectively? First, take the time to make up a target list of potential clients. Never bother sending postcards to people or businesses that will never have any use for what you do; that would be wasting your money. Once you have selected your target (and it will take a considerable amount of time to fine tune your target audience) you will need to create the message. What are you trying to accomplish with your postcard mailing?

Some businesses want to sell their products or services through the mailing. This is OK but often turns out to be just a one-shot deal that gets tossed. You will likely want to send out a series of postcards at specified intervals to make sure that your message is getting across to the potential user of your product or service. The first postcard should make a strategic announcement and the second and subsequent ones should be follow-ups.

Remember that by sending out postcards, you are looking to gain some brand recognition. If a business needs your service in the future, and you are doing regular postcard or other mailings, they will likely want to give you a call. This percentage will be low but you will have the branding you are looking for.

59.   *Flyers*

What benefits will you get from flyers?

Flyers are very different from postcards in that they convey product sales to the consumer. Safeway, Costco, Albertsons, and other grocery chains are excellent at putting out flyers. Many consumers will look at the specials and head out to purchase them either when they need them or simply to stock up. Do flyers work in this respect? Yes, or businesses would not be doing them. If you are not in a high-demand product line such as groceries, then instead of a multiple-page flyer you may want to stick to postcards or one-pagers that have more impact.

You can also be part of a flyer program that is offered by coupon book companies. Although you will be grouped together with other companies, your readership will likely be higher than if you try to go it alone. There are many really good coupon companies in most cities; the Yellow Pages, Chamber of Commerce directories, and other directory listings are the obvious first places to look. If your business is not consumer products but based on business to business, then flyers in a Chamber of Commerce newsletter will likely work better for you. You should find out ahead of time who they distribute their newsletter to: is it members only or does it go to all businesses within their postal code area? Businesses that belong to the Chamber will more than likely read all the flyers in the package and hopefully your response rate will be better than for a general mailing of the same material.

We have covered only a few ways to deal with flyers, but there are many more than we have room to mention. If you want to have flyers produced in any fashion, make them professional looking and have them professionally printed. The biggest cost is the design of your materials. Look for a professional designer who does good, fast work. This is not a place to skimp on the budget. Printers are not that expensive and the amount you pay will yield a better return on investment than if you do them yourself. Remember that it is your image that is out there all the time; you need to be consistent and look good!

60. *Lessons Learned*

What are the best ways to gain new contacts?

We have covered many ways to use the media to promote your business. You must ultimately decide which are best for your business. It may be all the ways we have mentioned or it may be only a few, but whatever you choose, you need to get a precise and clear message across to your potential buyers. Also make sure you form an excellent business relationship with any company before you do business together. You will want to create a solid business relationship, and you will want to do business for the long term and not just for a short-term project. A good business relationship makes it easier to be committed to what you are doing and get that commitment message across to your clients and potential clients.

How much to spend on public relations and promotion is entirely up to you. But once you decide how much to spend, plan to spend it wisely and not to flush your hard-earned dollars down the drain. I would advise you to do all of the above but do it in stages, and sometimes things like sponsorships will only come into play when you can afford it. The key is to get involved and stay involved; this consistency alone will reap rewards in the local community. When you walk into local businesses they will recognize you and be willing to talk. It is a give-and-take process that creates good solid business relationships; they just need to know that you are out there and can be depended on.

Also take advantage of PR (public relations) professionals who can turn your business ideas into news. For a list of these professionals you can check with consulting groups, Yellow Pages ads, and Web listings. Before you commit to a PR specialist, however, make sure you do your homework and find out what they have done for others in the past. This way you will not be disappointed with the results.

I decided that I wanted to be coached in PR. I wanted to know more about how to do it correctly while having a guiding hand. Many of you may know Jill Lublin (the writer of the Foreword to this book and author of the best sellers Guerrilla Publicity and Networking Magic), who has been speaking about PR for several years. It is Jill's coaching that has made me savvier and more PR aware. For more information on Jill Lublin and her coaching, visit her Web site, http://www.promisingpromotion.com.

Checklists

Sponsoring an Event

Name of the event

_____

Location: _____

Date and Time: _____

Intended Audience:

_____

_____

Total Cost of Sponsorship:

_____

_____

Publicity Potential:

_____

_____

Potential Business from the event:

_____

_____

Other Comments:

_____

_____

_____

_____

Donations

Name of the event: _____

Type of event: _____

Location: _____

Date and Time: _____

Intended Audience:

_____

_____

Total Cost of Donation:

_____

_____

Publicity Potential:

_____

_____

Potential Business from the event:

_____

_____

Other Comments:

_____

_____

_____

_____

_____

5. Speaking Engagements

61. *Expertise Defined*

Why do you have to be an expert
when getting speaking engagements?

The first thing you need to do before engaging in a speaking career is to define your expertise. I have seen so many speakers get relegated to the mediocre list because they claim they can talk on anything—"What would you like to hear?" Although I am not advocating sticking with one topic only, I do advocate that you be an expert in one field of your choosing. Do not try to be everything to everyone. The other day I came across a consultant who told me that he was in the application integration business and that he had some major customers. I asked, "How do you present your materials?" He explained that he simply worked with major vendors to make all their systems talk together. Then to my dismay he added "and I do training [which is OK] and I am also a management consultant to help management make decisions with processes and how to put them together." To each subsequent question I asked he replied "I do that too." Now I was totally confused. All of a sudden, I no longer viewed him as an expert and moved on.

You may find that you are more successful when you have defined your expertise, and you will stick to it! You may also provide other things to your clients, but when you are speaking to an audience, YOU are the expert and not a chameleon that changes its color with the changing smell of every new business opportunity. Remember to focus on what you do best and the rest will follow. When you secure a speaking engagement, attach a subject to it; don't leave it open. All of your materials should support your expertise even when it is customized for a client.

If you can clearly define your expertise, then business will be easier to obtain. People will come to know you in that field and ask your advice. Being an expert and defining it well is the first step to a speaking career within your field. Another thing you must be aware of is your audience and why they will listen to you.

62. Benefits to the Audience

What benefit do you provide the audience?

People should listen to you because you have an important message that will help them to improve their business or personal lives. They are there for no other reason. Yes, they will attend out of sheer interest, but these people will also have either business or personal reasons for being there. You are there to give advice that can be easily followed. Your advice will be taken as a proven statement even if you have never practiced the advice you give. How is this possible? For example, a university professor, will explain in detail business processes that are deemed to be the latest methods. Armed with these, the student feels assured of success. And yet, in reality, the professor has never tried these methods, but people try them because they are given by a recognized expert.

You must be certain that you absolutely, positively, without exception provide walk-away value. If you do not, everyone's time will have been wasted, including yours!

You will be listened to because you are offering solutions to problems that may exist in the marketplace. You will need to make sure that your topic is relevant in today's business environment and will attract an audience. Once you have determined the market, the actual presentation will be saleable and you will have the ear of every attendee. You must remember that they will listen and that you must convey a message that will solve a problem and also give an easily implemented solution. Do not tell lies or your career in speaking engagements will end abruptly. If you do tell lies, make sure you have insurance as a precaution in case you are sued.

Do not merely assume that a topic is salient—do your research to make sure it is. For example, I put on a free breakfast seminar in the San Francisco area a few months ago. I picked a topic that would be relevant to a society that was facing a downturn. The topic was the Seven Deadly Sins of Selling and the presenter was Ian Selbie. I informed everyone I knew (which was only a few hundred people) and I got a registration response of 117 attendees. It was an overwhelming success. The topic also had great walk-away value to the participants.

63. *Topic Value*

**What information can be used immediately
by the audience and what can they take away?**

Can you tell the audience in 30 seconds or less what you do and also give them three things that they can use immediately? Chances are you cannot. But if you cannot excite an enthusiastic response to how valuable your topic is, you are not likely to win over the audience. Not only do you need to think it is valuable—so must the audience. You will need to do some prior market research, even if it is only asking questions of your intended audience.

You need to know ahead of time that your chosen topic is of value to your audience and that they will be able to walk away afterwards feeling that they got value. There are three easy steps that you can take to make sure you are addressing your audience.

First, choose a topic with which you feel comfortable (of course, it may be one of several).

Second, pass several speech outlines to friends and local businesses to see if they are interested. Ask them which they would be interested in attending, and have them rank their choices in order of preference.

Lastly, e-mail your circle of influence and have them rate your titles and give suggestions. Once you have completed these steps, you are on the road to presenting something the audience will like.

If you do your research before spending money on advertising the event, you will get a better idea of what the market will bear. If you do a market survey through low-cost survey services such as surveymonkey.com, you will get measurable results. Analyze these results and take them seriously. If you ignore them and go by your own preferences, you risk having few attendees and wasting your own time and effort. The audience needs to have something tangible for their effort in listening to what you have to say.

64. *How Speaking Helps Business*

How do you gain contacts
from a speaking engagement?

The name of the game in speaking engagements is gaining more contacts to add to your list of potential clients. Speaking is only one way of attracting business. By providing a feedback form at the end of the talk, you have opened the door to potential clients. You need to ask how well you did, whether the material was relevant, and whether they want you to follow up with more information.

Be sure to ask for testimonials that you can use to promote your business and further your speaking engagements. When you follow up with feedback form inquiries, your calls will be readily accepted. The person responding has heard you speak about your expertise and may want to do further business. I look at speaking engagements as getting 100 or more cold calls completed all at the same time. Your contact list will grow and you will be able to offer other speeches to your audience.

Large or small, the size of the groups will not matter. The difference will be made by the content of your speech and the word-of-mouth reaction to the value you brought to the table. You can find your initial audience through volunteer organizations; these organizations are often looking for speakers. But you must be careful not to make your speech a commercial. If you do, you will not likely be invited back by other branches of their group nor will you likely do business with the members of the group. Remember, however you get your information out, you need to retain a list of the attendees for following up.

Once you have a few speeches under your belt, your contact list will grow considerably. You must be careful how you deal with the list: make sure you have each person's permission to keep him or her on your mailing list for future events. It is a slow process, but you will be better known for your integrity and your expertise rather than for being a selling machine.

65. *Getting Yourself Known*

What are the five best ways of
getting known in the speaking industry?

Getting known in the speaking industry does not happen overnight. You need to work at it bit by bit. Remember, you are an unknown in the beginning, even if you possess the expertise required for the audience.

First, you will need to speak to anyone who will listen.

Second, you will need to get feedback on how well you did and what the audience liked and what they thought needed improvement.

Third, do not take any of this feedback personally; use it as a tool to advance to the next stage in the speaking portion of your career.

Fourth, use constructive feedback as the basis for making improvements to your talk. Where there are conflicting comments make a judgment as to what should be the correct topic.

Last, you should have every speaking session videotaped, or at least audiotaped. You will need to review everything you said, even the stories of failures and successes. This step will enable you to make even further refinements. You can even tape yourself without an audience, but it is the audience reaction that you need to hear.

When you first begin, your audience is not likely to be well targeted. The likely reason is lack of the experience needed to more finely tune your definitions. In the beginning you are after constructive feedback, and when you are able to implement the feedback and fine tune the presentation, you are ready to further define your audience.

66. Defining Your Audience

Why should you be specific
about your intended audience?

Defining your audience is a matter of good business. Your topic may appeal to a diverse audience and a great many industries, but you will not maximize the response if you are too widely spread in your approach. Examine what you think your best audience will be. You should know the best vertical market or best industry for selling yourself and your company. It is this audience that will likely bring more business than if you spread yourself too thin. Remember that word of mouth is extremely valuable, and if you are in one market, the word will spread even faster.

The more industries you appeal to, the slower the word of mouth will be. There are too many variables and too many gaps to effectively leverage your speaking engagement. Say, for example, you are selling a training session on sales processes. The topic is relevant in every industry and every company you know could use the processes and techniques. You put on your first speech and get a great response on the follow-up. The problem is that you have to follow up and get referrals in too many areas and suddenly you cannot do an effective job of getting all that business. If you focus on one industry, yes you will follow up, but the word of mouth will also be working in your favor.

When you target your audience, they will start doing some of the work for you. In most industries it is a small world and people know each other and make recommendations (as long as they are not strong competitors with each other). The key is to have a common bond to the audience and capitalize on it.

67. *Speaking from a Publication*

Why write and get attention and loads of contacts?

Expertise can sometimes be defined by the articles, columns, responses, and books you write. It does not take a lot of effort to write the articles and columns, but it does take effort to write a book. Having a book behind your name shows your expertise. After all, you were able to write 300 pages on what it is you do and make references to your work through examples. What a good way to make cold calls and get people to attend your speaking engagements. Your sales efforts will be much easier once you are defined as the expert in the field. You will have something to refer to when speaking or going to a customer (or a potential customer) site.

You can readily quote the information from the book and use charts and graphs that are relevant to your topic. The audience will have an easier time believing what you say and will also likely want to meet with you for further business. You will not only sell books at the back of the room, you will also be selling your services, or that of your company, to a willing audience. Just think back to all the talks that you have attended, especially those that made the biggest impact on you. Very likely those speakers had a book for sale. I recently attended a talk by Jack Canfield and enjoyed his presentation and bought his book *Chicken Soup for the Soul*. Before purchasing the book, I would have said "Jack Who?"

By the way, Jack Canfield is an inspiration and his speeches are fantastic. He makes you realize that luck is a result of hard work and persistence! He is truly an expert in his field. His talks are also very informative.

68. Informative Speaking

Why should you do
informative talks to smaller groups?

Informative talks to smaller groups allow you more intimacy with the audience. You are able to more closely connect with their needs and their responses to your speech. You have something to say that is important not only to you but to the audience as well. They will take time to listen and not socialize as long as what you have to say is relevant to their pursuits. If you are not relevant, you must find a way to make your topic something they want to know about. You must make them aware of the importance of your topic. Suggest books they can read, and suggest ways they can use the content of your speech to their advantage to make improvements at work or at home. You want to make sure that you deliver something of value.

The point of an informative speech is not to sell yourself and make it an infomercial. The point is to inform the audience of a salient topic and give them information that they can use immediately. Once you have accomplished that task, gaining additional bookings will be easy. I have sat in many audiences and really enjoyed the speeches except when it came to the end and the speaker went into full commercial mode. A successful speaker who is making an informative speech does not do it; she simply lets the audience know she will be available for questions at the end of the speech.

An informative talk should also have some supporting materials so that it is easier for the audience to follow. Many speakers do not want to take the time or spend the money to provide unbiased handouts. The one thing I do is make sure they have a worksheet where they can jot down important information (which they keep for future reference). Be ready to dole out free information.

69. Give Free Advice

When is advice free and
when should you charge for it?

A question often asked is when to charge for information. There is no easy answer as it really depends on the situation. If you are doing a speech for a nonprofit organization, your advice can be pro bono (at no cost). I would have no difficulty sharing my expertise with such an organization, but I do draw the line when a for-profit organization asks for the same privileges. Nonprofits are exactly what the name says, and even though they do have money to spend in some areas, some free advice is good. The advice, however, should be given through formal channels. You should ask to work with their board of directors to see what help they actually need and then offer your services.

Remember that each person in a nonprofit also has a job in the community and may want to use your services or book you for an event as a speaker. The rule of thumb when giving free advice is to make sure you do not give the farm away. If you do, there is nothing more you can give to the business people in that organization. You should temper what you give so that the organization can move forward, but watch out for those organizations that tend to ask for more than you can give without doing harm to your own business. It is the additional information that you can charge for.

There will always be a fine line between giving free information and being exploited. If you are exploited, you will know it and the experience will give you a bad taste for some organizations, this is the exception, as most organizations do not operate in this manner. Give freely of your advice and make sure the information you give is being used as you intended.

70. Groups that Use Speakers

How do you find groups that are
in need of speakers (at no charge)?

Finding groups that use speakers is not difficult. I find that most organized service groups use speakers for their regular meetings. I have been a member of Rotary for nearly fifteen years. In that period of time, the clubs have used a speaker almost every week of the year. There are thousands of Rotary clubs all over the world. The most important thing to remember, especially for Rotary, is that the topic must be of interest to the members and that you cannot sell your services to the group. Many otherwise good speakers have not been recommended to other clubs as they tried to sell attendance to their speeches or training sessions.

I find that other groups such as Lions, Kiwanis, churches, PTAs, and so on all want to hear good talks and they do not want to be sold a bill of goods. You need to remember that your goal is to get your name known, not to sell. If one group likes your speech, they may give you referrals to other groups that would like to hear what you have to say. Another great place to offer a talk is at the Chamber of Commerce. Almost every town in North America has a Chamber. You will need to find out the protocols for putting on a talk, but most are open to new ideas and fresh topics. More often than not, you will find out about groups through your own networking efforts.

Some groups make it easy to get on the speakers list, but others will make it more difficult. They will want to know more about who you are, why you want to talk to the group, and how the topic fits for their members.

71. Guest Speakers Listings

How do you get your name on a speakers list?

Speaking experience is usually required before you can get placed on an organization's speakers list. Groups often want to know where you have spoken and will want to have referrals from a couple of the groups where you have already spoken. If you are just starting out, you will not have a list, but you have to start somewhere. You can explain to the group that you have not given any talks to their organization but you have trained others in your expertise. You may get a chance to fill a vacancy in their schedule for which they have no experienced speaker. Your topic, however, must fit their values; if it does not, you will not likely get on the list.

I have found that the list is somewhat sacred, and breaking into it is more difficult than is necessary. A good way to circumvent this difficulty is to put on a couple of seminars with a small audience at your own expense. This will give you the practice required and also give you an audience that can provide you with some referrals for additional speeches in the community. You can be creative in how you gain your experience, but the important thing to remember is that the letter of reference is what will make an impression and give you the chance to speak and be placed on the list. Do not give up if you are not accepted at first. Make plans to fulfill the criteria and try again.

Some speakers bureaus have lists of associations and groups that regularly need speakers. One such bureau is Walters International Speakers Bureau. You can find more information about this bureau by visiting: www.walters-intl.com.

Even if you belong to an organization, you may not readily get on the speakers list. I have run into this problem many times but managed to get the experience they required and then went to other clubs within my organization to get on their list.

72. Use Your Inner Circle

Who do you know who knows that you speak?

There is a famous saying, "It is not who you know but who knows you." This is so true. Take a look at who you know and also at others at your place of business, or clients that you have worked with or contacted in the past. Do they know who you are? Are they aware of what you do to promote yourself or your business? They should: This is all part of networking and forming business relationships. You need to make sure they remember you, even if they do not buy from you. Make them a part of your inner circle. Each of these people also has an inner circle—they will tell their friends and so on.

Remember the hair shampoo commercial a number of years ago that went, "Tell two friends, who will tell two friends, and so on, and so on . . ."? The image on the screen showed the talking heads multiplying. Not only did you get the buzz from the ad, it also encouraged you to pass it along.

You need to use your inner circle. List everyone you know (it will likely total well over 100 people), then make plans to inform every single one of them of what you are doing and why. Encourage them to tell all their friends (in the case of the shampoo ad, they only need to tell two, who should tell two). Your fame will spread rapidly.

You have likely heard the cliché that there are only six degrees of separation between any two people in the world. I know it is true for me because I have moved among countries and met people who knew people from my past or present life. In one country new to me I met a person who had gone to high school with my grandmother. You can use your inner circle to create excitement and further it by using the Web.

73. *Promoting on the Web*

Why use the Web for
promoting your speaking engagements?

Most people now agree that the Web offers a great deal of information, if not too much. Every business should have a Web site, even if only to tell people what you sell and where you are located. You may not want to sell chocolates over the Web for shipments of any distance in the hot summer, but you can tell people where your business is located and what specials you are running. I recently met a fellow who was getting married and needed to order a cake and find a wedding singer. Instead of looking in the Yellow Pages, he opted to do a Web search for local businesses to provide what he needed. He found only one baker out of 20 in his city that had a site. He could even choose the decorations over the Web. He bought from this store because it had provided convenience for him. He also located a singer in the same manner.

It does not matter what business you are in, the Web will provide you with a way to have an electronic brochure and a presence. I find that many of my clients want to know more about me before we meet; they look at my Web site to determine whether I have the expertise they are looking for. I, in turn, look for the potential clients' site to learn more about what they do. Do not dismiss the Web as not for you simply because you are not savvy. There are plenty of designers who will put up a simple site for you in a couple of days' time. You must, however, provide them with the content.

An important advantage to having your own Web site is that it will allow you to have your own e-mail address, at your own domain name. Not only does this make you look more professional, you will also never need to change your e-mail address again! Think of the savings in printing cards, never mind the consistency of the image you create for yourself.

Once you have a Web site, try to get links to it everywhere you can. One way is to join an organization that has a member site and will list you in the price of your membership. Chambers of Commerce offer this feature and are a good place to start.

74. Chambers of Commerce

Why are Chambers a good launching pad?

Chambers provide you with more ways to get to know the business community than most organizations. I was once elected President of a Chamber, and during my tenure the Board strived to get businesses involved with one another. One of our mandates was to make sure that we had opportunities for networking and socializing both between members of one Chamber and with other Chambers as well. We often put on professional development talks. A good example of how a Chamber helps the business community is through its involvement with the city in which it is located. The Chamber gives you a voice in the community and further aids you by allowing you to advertise in its publications.

Many people have told me that their Chamber is useless because the businesses that belong to it are too small. This may be true in some respects, but Chambers also have large corporations as members, and their presence is especially important if they are involved in the community. For example, the Chamber in San Ramon, California, counts Chevron Texaco as a member, and they are deeply involved in the community. The Chamber recently sponsored awards at which two employees from Chevron Texaco were honored for their commitment to the community at large. You should never downplay an organization that provides so much service to the business community.

Chambers also offer a venue for speakers. They will often put on a professional development series for members. Even though these events usually draw only 25 or 30 people, those that attend often tell others about the success of the event. You really need to get involved and make the most of what is there for you. Chambers are also willing to promote their own members.

75. *When You Can Expect to Be Paid*

> Now that you have all the contacts you can possibly use, when can you expect to get paid for speaking or other business engagements?

You have done your job and spoken to many nonprofits and Chambers, your name is getting well known and you have even been hired and paid to do a couple of speeches. Now it is time to look further down the road. You can continue to self-promote your speaking, but you will also need to use other tools. One tool would be the use of a speakers bureau.

These bureaus will want a great deal of information from you. They will also want a cut of your speaking engagement fees, and they may want a host of additional monetary incentives. If you choose a speakers bureau, make sure it will promote you and not take you to the cleaners. There are many very good bureaus, but you must do your research.

Another excellent avenue for speaking engagements is through professional associations. If you belong to the National Speakers Association, The Association of Management Consultants, or any other such trade organization, you will have opportunities to put on a seminar at their conventions.

This is another good way to become known for your expertise and another way to network with professionals in your field. Remember that every contact you make should go into your contact list even if you do not use them initially.

Checklists

One of the keys to getting speaking engagements is to make sure you know your own expertise.

List at least five areas where you feel you are an expert:

_____

_____

_____

_____

_____

_____

_____

From your list of expertise determine which three areas will most help your business grow:

_____

_____

_____

From the list above, determine why anyone would listen to a speaker on that subject – this is a list of benefits of each topic and not a list of features (use a separate page if you need more room):

_____

_____

_____

_____

_____

According to the benefits – who will be your target audience?

_____

_____

Name at least 3 groups that would be an ideal speaking venue for the topic(s) you have selected:

_____

_____

_____

_____

What publications, articles, or other proof do you have that puts YOU as the expert for these topics?

_____

_____

_____

_____

List the writing you plan to do in the next 6 months to support YOUR expertise:

_____

_____

_____

_____

_____

_____

6. Relationships

76. *Relationship Defined*

What makes a business relationship?

What really makes a business relationship? This can be very hard to define as it goes beyond just meeting a person and chatting about something you have in common. Most business relationships are developed over a period of time—very rarely do they happen instantly. I once met a person at a Rotary function who was an ideal business partner for me. I spent some time chatting with him at the event; we exchanged cards and agreed to meet on another occasion to discuss our mutual needs. Approximately three months went by before we had a chance to reconnect. At that time we discovered that we had a common interest in movie going and both our spouses did as well. We decided to go to the movies as a group that weekend. This was the beginning of the business relationship. We had something in common that we both enjoyed. Even so, here it is two and a half years later and I am just starting to do business with this person. This story simply means that you do not make instant business relationships; they must be nurtured.

In another example, the process was much quicker. I met a CPA at a networking and problem-solving meeting and we instantly discovered that I had some services he required. We agreed to meet to discuss the project. We also created a business relationship in that I agreed to help his son write his first book. This relationship took a period of two months to form, not two years. What really makes a relationship is a common interest or goal and a fit for what you each have to offer. A business relationship is not a one-way street—there must be give and take or it will fall apart.

If you have the necessary expertise, the relationship will develop more quickly than if you have to search for something that will click. Personal interests, the direction in which you want to take your business, even your focus all come into play.

77. *Benefits of Knowing You*

Why are business relationships
formed with certain people?

If you go to a networking meeting and look around the room, can you tell which individuals you would like to converse with? You will be likely to gravitate toward those who are engaged in conversation and have an enthusiasm about them. If you see people sitting around looking like wallflowers, you will not be as likely to want to find out more about them.

You should make sure that you are listening to what others have to say so that you can decide whether you have a common interest. Another point is to make sure that you are able to talk to them on their level, not yours. Discuss many things including hobbies and activities to find that common bond.

You need to give people a reason to listen to you and what you have to offer. In the long run, you want to develop a business relationship first and do business later. I was recently at a networking club that was new to me where all those present chatted with one another like old friends. Instead of feeling left out, I walked around and listened to what they were saying and, if I had some experience in that subject, I found a way to interject and add my two cents. This technique gave me instant acceptance into the group. I had formed an instant common bond. I also went back to my office and sent an e-mail to each of the members I met and asked for an appointment to discuss how we could find leads for each other. Not one person turned me down.

78. Drop the EGO

When does your ego get in the way?

Let's go back to that networking meeting and scan the room again. Did you notice the person who never stops talking? He is the one who is talking about how great his business is and how great his services are. He even gets bold enough to take your card and to try to set up an appointment with you to sell his services. This is the person who has placed his ego in front and although he is enthusiastic about what he does, he is also enthusiastic about hearing himself talk. He has not spent any time listening to what others have to offer, nor has he asked any questions. This is the person around whom you cannot get a word in edgewise, and if you do, he always turns the subject back to himself. You do not need to avoid such a person, but you must in some manner help him drop the ego and get on with what he came for, to network.

If you spend more time listening than talking, you will get farther with business relationships, but do not let the person talking the entire time take the floor. After all, such people are not talking about what they need in the way of services and products to move their business forward; they are simply pushing themselves. To be successful in gaining some business relationships—and you should always try to develop at least one at each event—listen to what others say and encourage them to talk about their business concerns. You must put your best foot forward at all times and listen to the needs of others. If you can offer a solution to someone's problems and set up a further meeting for additional discussion, then you are much farther ahead. The goal is to gain a business relationship, not to sell your services.

Business relationships can be fairly easy to form if you do not spend your time selling yourself at an event. Yes, others will want to know what you have to offer and how you fit, but the goal is simply to start a relationship.

79. Who Makes the Best Partner?

How do you find the best business partners?

Finding a good business partner—that is, an outside partner, such as an alliance—requires an amount of due diligence. This simply means you will need to look at all aspects of the other person's business and sometimes a bit of her personal life. You will need to find a common thread with the potential partner and then spend time developing the relationship before embarking on any kind of partnership that will tie you financially to the person. I have heard so often that partnerships do not work. When I dig into the reason, it turns out that each of the parties liked each other and decided to create the relationship on an emotional level. A partnership will very rarely fall apart so readily if you have done your homework and have acquired enough information about the financial background of the potential partner in business and at home. Credit ratings will often tell a great deal about an individual.

I have a business relationship with a person who only hires people with a credit rating over 650. To him, this number indicates that the person he is hiring respects his rating, and will likely not take advantage of the company. He also believes that people with a good credit rating will tend to be more loyal to the job as they do not need to seek other employment or do side deals to make up the difference between their salary and what they owe.

There are many other ways besides credit rating you can use to determine who makes the best business partner. Among them are the community activities they are involved in and the organizations they have joined. A person who helps others is more than likely going to help the partnership.

80. *Getting to the Right People*

Where do you find the right
people for a business relationship?

Finding the right people may not be as difficult as you might think. Quite often they are in your neighborhood and within your inner circle. There are three things that you can do to find the person with the right fit for a business relationship.

First, define the ideal customer: Identify the criteria of such a customer and list, in some detail, the traits that satisfy those criteria. Be sure to also identify the industry or industries in which these traits exist.

Second, list all those organizations in your geographic area that fit the profile you have just created. This process will be ongoing, as once you have identified local firms, you will want to expand the list to those beyond the immediate locality.

Third, arrange the list in order of preference, then start with number one. Do some further research to determine who you need to meet. Spend some time discovering what events they attend and what community activities they are involved in, then find a way to get yourself introduced as an expert in your field. This process will take a lot of energy, but you do not have to make an exhaustive list at the outset, you can make it manageable by starting with the top five businesses where you see a fit and where you think you can get an introduction. Remember that people in your inner circle may have a tie to someone in those organizations.

The important thing in getting to the right people is to educate yourself about their business so that you can tailor your services to fit their needs. If, for example, they have a fleet of cars and you discover a way to save them money on fuel, you will have something they may wish to purchase. You do need to get that introduction first, as a cold call will only yield a 1 to 2 percent return on your time.

81. Pipeline or Downline

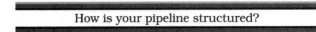

How is your pipeline structured?

Most of you must know what the sales pipeline is. It keeps track of where you are in the sales process with prospects and customers. You keep track of all your activities, meetings, and business deals. Your pipeline is what keeps your business going. It is a lot like a funnel: At the large end you need to do lots of activities that will generate a slew of interested contacts; some of these move down the funnel and become coached; of these, a few get qualified, and even fewer go on to be selected and finally closed. Once you have a customer, the tendency is to spend your time at that end of the funnel fulfilling the work. When the job is done, you turn around and there is no more work waiting; you go back to the other end of the funnel and start all over.

The important lesson here is that you need to keep a balanced flow within your pipeline so that you do not run out of clients at the end of the day. Have you ever been in a situation where you were working with one client who took up enormous amounts of your time and you had no time to do your marketing activities? And the client without warning canceled the project and you were left without any work and nothing in the pipeline? This is the worst thing that can happen to a business. You should always have Plan B and Plan C and Plan D, and so on in the wings at all times.

There are several stages in the pipeline, and you must remember to work on keeping things flowing through. If you get a customer who tends to eat all your time, make sure he understands that you must take one day or half a day every week to work on your own marketing efforts. You can suggest that the client extend the project over a longer period of time so that your needs are also met. You will find that most clients want their project to have first priority and that you will need to schedule your time around your own marketing activities. The important thing to remember is that you must always fill the pipeline.

Your need to fill the pipeline while being tied up in other projects may seem to present difficulties, but you will find that a number of networking opportunities are held either early in the morning or in the evening. Some events are held at the lunch hour. Take advantage of this and set new client meetings around meal times. Don't let your business dry up; always work toward finding new relationships that can lead to future projects.

82. Business Similarities

Why does a good business relationship
rely on having some common business objectives?

As you attend networking events, you will gradually find ways that make it easy for you to mingle and be heard. Your message will need to be clear, focused, and consistent each time. You will find that many of the people you met at one event will attend others you go to. These are the people that you will likely form a kind of bond with. It is these people you can work with to brainstorm on the best networking events to attend and to identify those that have not panned out.

This is also a way to start new business relationships. If you had not found anything in common with them before, you now have something to discuss. You can ask questions as to the type of business they are looking for and who their best customer is. You can also find out more about their business objectives and how they may mesh with what you are doing at the present time. The ultimate goal here is to get to the first appointment to explore possibilities. They may want to do business with you as much as you want to do business with them

Once you focus on similarities between each company and commonalities between individuals, the business relationship has an opportunity to form. You are not selling at this point; you are simply trying to establish a good business relationship. Each of you may try a little of what the other has to offer in order to test the waters before the relationship can be solidified.

Business "pain" is flaunted regularly in marketing and sales circles and sometimes has very little meaning. Most organizations will not reveal their pain to anyone except an insider. If you are able to form a solid business relationship within the company, then you will be closer to finding out what improvements the company desires.

83. Six Degrees

How far away is the person you need to meet?

We have spent some time discussing your inner circle and have suggested that you take time to list all of the people whom you know and who KNOW YOU. This inner circle is where you start your search for someone who knows a person you need to meet. You will need to take time to contact everyone on your list with news and make sure you ask for referrals. I know this is somewhat difficult as I hate asking friends and acquaintances for anything. The best way to get support for your endeavors and get the introductions you want is to put on an event. The event can be a party, a celebration of your new product line or service, a business seminar, or any other thing that will bring people to you for face-to-face interaction.

Suggest that your friends bring others who they know will be interested in what you have to offer. Your friends are more likely to invite and introduce you to others in a social setting than on the phone, which they might feel puts them on the spot. Use your inner ring to get to your outer ring. Using Web technology to find these relationships is sometimes a necessity. Try LinkedIn.com and see what it can bring you. When you do decide to put on an event, be very specific about who you want to attend and try to tailor the invite list to suit your business needs. As mentioned before, I put on a seminar and invited business people to get some free information and I paid for the breakfast. It took six months to follow up on all the leads and get appointments with those who were interested. I even got referrals from attendees who thought someone they knew could use me.

Events will go a long way to tap into existing relationships and expand your inner circle. To get people to attend, you must have something of value to offer. Your offering must also be consistent.

84. A Consistent Message

Why does consistency in the message
have an effect on how the
business relationship is formed?

Your message to others must be consistent. You need to define your expertise and develop your elevator pitch. Do not go to events and change your description of what you do just because the person you are talking to needs something just outside your sandbox. Remember, that person is at a networking meeting as well. If you tell one person something and another person something else, they may talk to each other about you and then wonder what you really do. This is not the picture you want painted of yourself. You are the one who needs to focus; define what you do and keep that message consistent. Even as you develop your pitch, you must try to avoid generalizations. If I say "I am a management consultant," people will not think me an expert in anything, as my title says I am a generalist with no specific focus.

If on the other hand I say that "I am a business mechanic and I help organizations maintain, repair, and tune up their business processes in relation to marketing and sales," then I have shown that I have expertise and they can more readily relate to what it is I do. My message will always be the same. What I do in reality may push the envelope, but I will make sure that it fits in with my business description. You need to make sure that you are consistent with the message. By the way, maintain that consistency also in your company's printed materials as well as on your Web site.

A consistent set of messages to identify who you are and what you do will draw more people and organizations to you. They will have the understanding of how you could fit into their organization and how they can use your services.

85. *Nurturing the Relationship*

Who is responsible for
maintaining the business relationship?

Nurturing a business relationship will take effort on your part and effort on the part of the other person. If you feel the business is worth having, then you must take the time to make sure you are in touch on a regular basis. I call these contacts touch points. Each touch point you have with the client is a point in your favor. Most people like to keep the channels open for conducting current projects or for future business. I know a CEO of a company called Olympia Funding in Pleasanton, California, who has a policy of sending out personal messages to all his contacts at the end of every month. These are usually in the form of postcards with good information. He also has his staff send "letters from the heart" each quarter. Through this touch point activity and a few other touch points, he is able to do millions of dollars of business without making cold calls. He has the referrals pouring in.

This CEO knows the value of maintaining the business relationship. If a multimillion dollar corporation takes the time to keep in contact, then you know that you must also put a plan together that creates an awareness of you. It is WHO knows YOU and not who you know that ultimately matters. At your next networking event, gather business cards and then make contact through e-mail to set up an appointment with each to find common ground. Ask those who give you their card if you can add them to your mailing list for your newsletter containing up-to-date information that may help them. Take the time to work on being in touch; the results are amazing.

Another good way to nurture a relationship is to find out interests and keep a record of what those interests are. When you come across something of interest, send it to the person, who will remember this when it comes to sending out an RFP. It is in your best interest to know more about them than they do about you.

86. *Know More About Them Than...*

Why do research and education play
an important part in the business relationship?

Have you ever attended a business briefing or meeting without reading the materials ahead of time? I know I have, and I also know that I felt like a fool when asked a question. It was up to me to be informed about the meeting and to read the information, and I neglected to do so. When you attend a meeting for a potential client, you will often find that they have not read much about you and have not done their research. Make sure that it is the other party wearing those shoes and not you. Find out all you can about their business so that you have a fairly accurate understanding of their potential business needs. You may also discover some problems they have in keeping up with the competition or other items of interest that you can discuss at the meeting. You want to make sure that you are better informed about their business than they are about you.

Once you have gained an understanding of their business, spend some time in the meeting asking relevant questions about how they tackle certain aspects of their business. You are working toward forming a bond and a business relationship here, and not trying to sell your products or services. Have them speak on what they do best and what they think the competition's weaknesses are. Also give free advice on some possible solutions that you can discuss in detail further down the road. The main goal of the first meeting is an introduction and to get to the second meeting, nothing more and nothing less.

You may discover in your research that the company has many strong points, but at the same time some weaknesses may be revealed. Do not play on those weaknesses, but play to their strengths. If the weaknesses get in the way, that may be your signal to book time with another client.

87. Annoyances

When do annoyances in a
relationship create problems?

When you first set up your business relationship, you did an amount of research that should have identified some of the potential problems that could arise. No matter how much information you have, little annoyances will also crop up. You need to look at the reasons why alliances fail and try to solve problems before they get too big. Have you likely worked for a client who drives you up the wall and back down the other side but you keep working with him because you need the money? I am sure most of us have been in that position and were so happy when that relationship finally broke up. You felt that you were finally free and able to do what you do best somewhere else. Or, on the other hand, you fell into panic because you had no income anymore. In either situation, the annoyances leave a bad taste for that type of business and you will likely seek clients in other industries.

This is not the best solution. You should always try to discover what is annoying you and why. It could be that the company is not aware of how annoying one of their procedures is or that there are problems in completing projects. If you have a good business relationship, you will be able to approach that person and let her know there are problems that need to be solved before a quality job can be completed.

In most cases, people are reluctant to bring up problems for fear they will be blamed and sent on their way. If you have a solid business relationship, there should be no fear in bringing up the event that is causing pain. If you cannot resolve the problem, you must decide whether the frustration is worth hanging onto or whether it is time to wrap up your end of the contract early. If you want to preserve your sanity, follow up with the problems, try to come to a solution that works, and if you cannot, move on.

Your method of communication when experiencing problems on a project will reflect how you conduct business. It is ultimately important that you act in a professional manner no matter what the outcome.

88. *Never Burn a Bridge*

Why should you always maintain rapport
with a business even when you are parting ways?

It is human nature to get angry and rant and rave about what is not going well at work. Many of us spend time socializing and gossiping with the main topic being what the current problems are and who is responsible. Although venting may yield a certain satisfaction, it is not the way to gain further business with a client.

When a relationship is no longer working, always debrief the other party with your findings, give suggestions for solving the problems, and walk away with a handshake. It is this professionalism that will gain you respect and possibly more business in the future. Remember that the business relationship must be preserved in order for you to move forward with other business. You do not need to add skeletons to your closet, as you never know when someone you want to do business with will know the client that you just concluded your relationship with.

Never burning a bridge is one of the most difficult things to do in business. In the past, I have burnt a few and have always later regretted it. But no more: I have since made it a point to say that things are not working out, let's go our separate ways but remain friends. This may sound less than reasonable, but sooner or later that person will have direct influence over whether your company is selected or not. If you have burnt the bridge, you can be assured that the business will go elsewhere.

I know this from experience. I once had a contract with a government agency to provide certain services. Although my work was exemplary, the person who was in effect my "boss" kept changing what was wanted. As a result, I quit in frustration and let him know how I felt. Doing this felt good at the time, but a couple of years later I was bidding on a big project and, to my horror, this very same person was making the final decision. I did not get the business even though we had the best offering.

The worst thing for me was the egg on my face: I had done all the work of presenting a proposal and I had my staff ready to go. Explaining to them why we lost the bid was not an easy task, but we all learned from it and, believe me, I will go to any length to keep a relationship and forgo the work.

89. Getting Involved

When do you need to get more involved with
the day-to-day activities of your business partner?

The best business relationship is one in which the client cannot tell whether you are a contractor or an employee. Working alongside the client, you are the one who offers solutions to problems. Such relationships take time to develop, but if your expertise helps make them a profit, clients will be more open to having you "on staff." To place yourself in this position, you need to possess an expertise that the client does not have. You also must make sure that you have a working knowledge of their processes and procedures. You are not there to make policy decisions but to push them in the right direction when your technical expertise is required. I know a company in the aeronautics industry that works so closely with one of its clients that it helps them design their airplanes and gives them advice on where they can save money and improve their processes.

This contractor company is so ingrained in the client organization that upper management takes them for granted. The main problem they are facing is getting in front of the decision makers so that they can do more business. This is not a bad problem to have, but you still have to maintain your identity. Companies that work this well together have gone past the dating game and are now well matched and have a solid long-term relationship. I am not suggesting that you want to work for only one company; I simply mean that you need to get close enough to your client that you know how you can be of value and let them know where they can make improvements.

Getting involved with other businesses is the best way to cement a relationship and to ensure longevity with the projects. It will also eliminate the threat of competition as potential competitors are unknowns and you know the client's trade secrets intimately. You need to bond the relationship to make sure you stay in the client's mind.

90. *How to Bond a Relationship*

When should you create a foundation
in order to solidify a business relationship?

Before you bond any business relationship, you need to make sure that the relationship is one that you both want to have. No relationship is a one-way street; it must work in both directions. You must have expertise that the client needs and the client must have the resources to reward you for those services. Never try to downplay your offerings with deep discounts, changes in what you provide, or any other thing that will decrease your value. The client must value what you have to offer through payment. Pro bono work in the beginning to prove yourself will only harm you and the relationship you are trying to cultivate. If you do free work, the value of your expertise will be limited and the customer will likely not want to pay your going rate.

If the client values what you have to offer and is willing to enter into a contractual agreement for services, the relationship is worth bonding. You can bond a relationship by offering to work on a value-based fee system which will not limit access to you during business hours and also give you freedom to conduct your work within the time frame given. This type of system also prevents micromanagement of how you spend your time. For example, if you charge an hourly rate, the basis of your value has changed to "how many hours can I afford?" and "I want to know what that person is doing every day for the money I am paying." A value based fee system will allow you to bond the relationship.

Checklists

How many business relationships do you currently have? _____

List at least five businesses that you would like to target for business over the next few months:

_____

_____

_____

_____

_____

If you know, who is the name of the person that you need to form a solid business relationship with:

_____

_____

_____

_____

What do you need to know about each of the people you listed in order to form a type of "bond"?

_____

_____

_____

_____

What things do you like to do and discuss? List any of these items that can help you form a business relationship:

_____

_____

_____

NOTES

7. Power Pad

91. The Power Page

How do we keep track of our business deals?

If you are working with only one or two deals, keeping track of them is a simple matter. However, most of us have far more than two deals on the plate and even more coming down the pipeline. It is sometimes quite difficult to keep track of all the details and remember who said what to whom. You need to keep track of the names of people on each deal or project and what their responsibilities are. Unfortunately it is time consuming and you can often miss out on important proposals or calls that you need to make. Keeping track of details is necessary, and keeping accurate records is also of prime importance. It is sometimes advantageous to keep track of details that are outside the norm, such as what other services a company needs that you do not provide. You can use this information to refer others into the account.

There are many techniques that you can use to keep on top of the situation. You can purchase CRM (Customer Relation Management) software to handle the contact details plus a host of other information. Using the computer to track information does not have to be onerous or difficult; it simply has to be planned into your day. I use my computer extensively for everything I do, but I do not carry it to meetings with me; I carry a simple paper notebook for each client and keep meticulous notes. I then transfer the important points to the computer system and have it refer to my paper journal for further details (I number my journals and file them for later use). Appointments, phone numbers, managers' names, titles, project roles are all on the computer system. Detailed notes with dates are on my power page, or paper journal, in my notebook.

We will go into more detail about the power page a little later in the chapter. Right now let's walk through the various components that are necessary for keeping the details straight and continuing to nurture our business relationships.

92. Information Plan

What is in an information plan?

An information plan should consist of five areas, each addressing certain aspects of any potential deal and containing information that must be gathered. Let's look at each of the areas and see what you need to learn about the client.

First, gather the contact information about the decision maker including the personality type (we deal with personality types later in the book). You also need information on other levels within the company. Who is the influencer in the situation, her name, title, and to whom she reports, plus her personality type? You also want to know about anyone else who will be able to sway the decision whether to hire your company or purchase your products. You now have the first step in the process.

Second, information about sales volume should be gathered. This information is readily available if the company is publicly traded. If it is a privately held company, you may need to find other sources of information. The information is not hard to get, as most companies like to boast about their sales record.

Third, you will want to know what type of problems they are encountering. In other words, what is their business pain? Make note of some solutions that you can provide, but make sure that they are not carved in stone until after the meeting with the client.

Fourth, you will need to know something about their customers: Are they happy? What do they see as the company's strengths and weaknesses? Once again you may have to ask for some leads or wait until you do an analysis of their perceived value.

The fifth and last thing to record is birthdates, anniversaries, special interests, and hobbies for each of the contacts. This last piece will help cement the bond. You will have created a place for a touch point with the client that is outside the scope of the contract. They will think of you when a similar project comes along. You can generally gather most of this information informally such as at a lunch meeting. You can take mental notes while listening. Record your notes on your power page after you leave the meeting, but do reiterate the major points that you heard before moving on.

93. *Consultative Approach*

What do we mean by a consultative approach?

When you hear the word "salesman," it usually brings to mind someone who is pushy and will not take no for an answer. If you told a prospective client you were in sales, you would likely turn him off. Yet, all businesses rely on their sales force to bring dollars into the firm. The sales force makes the company run, as there would be no inflow of cash without them. So how do you attack such an image problem? The answer lies in the approach that you take when networking. Your job, even though it may be sales, is to act as a consultant and try to find the perfect fit for the client. This approach is called consultative selling and it works very well for anyone who tries it.

I once worked with a company that relied exclusively on the consultative approach. The company was a major supplier of telephone services, and they had made the switch to consultative selling in order to fill seats in their very large training facility. Too many people who wanted to take the courses initially found them too expensive. This was mainly due to the initial method they used for selling. When the company sales staff switched to a consultative role, the number of paying trainees increased by 30% or more. The company no longer "sold seats," they sold a concept that included training and follow-up to ensure what they taught was implemented.

This leads back to the idea of pricing your services based on value rather than an hourly rate. Follow-up is the key to the success of this method. You need to plan the follow-up needs and to spend time caring for the customer—it is not something you throw in to make the sale.

Record any discussions on how the follow-up process will work for you. Also write a planned set of dates on your power page and enter them into your CRM software for milestone triggering. If you promise anything to the customer, write it down, put it in your calendar, and follow through with your promises. Nothing turns clients off more than being ignored.

94. *Win/Loss Analysis*

What to do when you win or lose.

You have given your elevator pitch, you have met with the customer, and you have identified her business value proposition and business pain as well. Now you have jotted down your proposal, detailing all of the information you have gathered. The proposal outlines the way you see the problem and the way the client sees the problem (if you used a consultative approach, you will be able to see the problem from the client's point of view). You have also given the client some options for proceeding on the project. Now you sit and wait.

In reality, you wait only a couple of days so that the client has time to read the proposal and digest it; then you follow up for a discussion of the proposal. The meeting is set and now you will answer questions about what it is you will do for the client.

The client will likely accept most of what you propose, but there is a chance that the proposal will be shelved until a later date. If this happens, you have not convinced the client of your value. You will need to go back and see what part of the process was not in your favor. The best way to do this is to ask the client what you could have done better in order to win the business. This follow-up will bring responses that range from a budget cut, an influencer wanted the competition in place, or your proposal was out of line. Chalk it up as a learning experience, but make sure you continue to keep the client in the loop as part of your inner circle. It comes back to never burning your bridges and being extremely professional at all times.

When you lose a deal, it is important that you take time to debrief the client to learn why you did not get the contract. If you win, what happens? You usually simply go on with the project. But it is important that you also debrief the client even when you win the deal. You will learn what earned you the contract and also what areas the client would like to see improved.

95. *Power Page*

What other information
do you need to keep track of?

Now you have the deal and you have completed your debriefing session and are ready to start on the project or sell the products to the client. End of story? No! Now more than ever you need to work closely with the client and to keep your power plan in place; the power plan is part of your power page and should detail how you plan to keep the client in the loop as the project moves forward. It should also include other touch points that may allow you to expand on the current project or even identify another project that will spin off from the current one. If you are selling product, you will want to make sure you schedule delivery dates, dates to follow up on the quality of the shipment, ideas for helping them use the product more effectively, and other points of follow-up.

The power page will help you mark milestones and times when you need to show the client how much you care about their business. It is important that you make sure the client is happy at all times. Do not pester the client by scheduling too many touch points, but do contact them at least once a month; sometimes twice a month is a good balance. If you contact them weekly, they might feel that you are being too pushy. It is a fine balance, but if you are doing your homework, you will be able to determine how often is acceptable to the client. Just make sure you record all this information on your power page and then add the dates to your calendar.

Recording information can be the bane of the salesperson. I know I hate the paperwork and cannot stand doing things twice, once in written form and once on the computer. If you are more comfortable with just the computer, then take a laptop to your meetings. I find that the noise of typing and the fact that I am not looking the customer in the face is a real distraction and can lead to lags in conversation and waste considerable time, whereas jotting notes in a notebook does not interrupt the discussion flow.

96. Profile

Why should you analyze your potential client?

At first glance, this topic may seem a little out of order. But you will find that although you have done your homework before getting the contract and already know a fair amount about your client, you do not know everything that is pertinent to the job. Once you have the project underway you will be adding to your knowledge of the client. In other words, you will be getting to know them more intimately than before. The information you had at the beginning is what the organization allowed you and the public in general to know. Now you are in a position to increase that knowledge and add to the client profile. This information will take time to accumulate; it will not present itself in its entirety right at the beginning of the project. Your performance it is what will make it surface.

Acquiring additional information is not the same thing as being a spy and learning the inner secrets of the organization. You are simply being aware of your surroundings and seeing what influences the results of the project. Company profile information should be kept separately from the project information. If you uncover facts or politically charged influences within the company, these factors will need to be addressed in some fashion. This does not mean that you are ratting on others. It simply means that you are concerned for the success of the project and need to have these issues addressed. Do not let anything pass you by; record it in the profile and deal with it head-on.

Setting meetings as issues arise is the most effective way to address potential risks to a project; setting regular meetings will often get in the way of progress, so schedule them only when there are a number of issues to discuss. If there is only one and it is not major, try to wait until you have recorded several. However, if an emergency is discovered, then, yes, schedule a meeting immediately to solve the problem.

97. *Contacts*

Any level will do, but where does the money flow?

Part of the power plan is making sure you have all the necessary contact information within a company. It is one thing to have the CEO's information, as he or she is the decision maker, but it is quite another to have the information on others that you may be working with directly. You will not likely work directly with the CEO on any project or product purchase; you will be referred to the appropriate person. Gather the same information on others as you gathered on the CEO. You will need to know the personality type to give you that inside edge, and also how much influence each person has on the decision to make a purchase; you may find that these other contacts have an authorized spending limit following a set of guidelines.

You want to make sure you target the correct person once the deal is made. These contacts will often have an inside edge on up-and-coming projects where you might be of use. They may even get additional funds in order to buy from you. I had a client who was limited to $10,000 on any purchase order, and my services for the quarter were to be $32,000. Instead of having to fill out the paper work and get additional approvals, he simply made four separate contracts for me, each with its own start dates, milestones, and project completion time. It worked well for him as he did not need additional approval to continue the project, and it worked for me as I was paid sooner than otherwise.

Having a person in the company at the right level for approving projects and purchases will make a difference between making the sale and knocking on the next door. You need to form a close relationship with that person and make sure he or she is completely satisfied with your work.

98. *Business Pain*

What are the company's
most challenging business issues?

Every company has business pain, but the pain does not necessarily mean that the company is not succeeding. Pain can be anything from a minor dent, as when a marketing event does not produce the anticipated results, to a major process issue, as when reporting is not accurate. As you set out to find your customer's business pain, you should remember that you are not necessarily looking for huge issues; rather you are looking for issues that hurt the profitability of the company.

For example, I once worked with a company that sold calculators. The company had a process in place that automatically ordered more calculators when the computer showed only one left in stock. On one occasion they were getting rid of old stock and ordering newer models for sale. When the old stock's level hit one, the order system automatically sent a P.O. to accounting for fifty more of that model. Sometimes the accounting department would catch the error and other times it went through. It became a real annoyance to return back-orders they did not need. The computer system was a business pain.

Instead of fixing the system, they relied on the accounting department to make the adjustments. Not until the suppliers started to get annoyed did they recognize this problem as something that needed to be fixed. Sometimes it takes an organization a long time to admit that they have a business pain that needs to be rectified. More often than not, they will not know that they have the pain; they will only feel a dull ache.

All the minor aches of a company should be recorded somewhere on your power page. You are not likely to put them into a CRM system, but they can give you leverage if you have a simple solution.

99. *Value Proposition*

How do you define your own value proposition?

Every company has a value proposition: a statement of the company's perceived value to its clients. Often a company will have one perception at the executive level, another at the sales level, and even a third at the client level.

Value propositions need to be aligned so that the customer is getting a consistent message. If the value proposition is not aligned you will have different levels, different directions, and different speeds that are not aiming at the same results. If you take the time to find out what others are saying about your value and compare that to what you think your value is, you may be quite surprised that the two values are not the same. If you aim to keep happy customers, then you must change your value proposition to match that of the customer's perception.

I have a colleague who was working on a company assessment to find out if the value proposition from the executive level, sales level, and customer level were the same. He found that this company and others of similar size ($100 million in sales) do not align their value proposition to what the customer sees as the value. In fact, he found that what they thought was the best part of their company was actually not very important to the customer.

Ask yourself what your value proposition *should* be, not what *you* think it should be. Work with your clients to achieve an alignment of perceived values and actual value. Keep a record of everything that is said about the company and its value. Help your customers and your staff understand what they bring to the table and you will likely win more business.

100. Revenue History/Plan

How do you keep track of clients' revenues?

The client's revenue history is vital information that you need to record in your power page. Keeping track of client revenues should not be done in a paper format; it should be recorded electronically. It is too easy to make mistakes when calculating by hand. The results of the electronic data entry can then be recorded into your power page. You need to date these numbers as they can change quite rapidly and you will want to know if there is a growth pattern. You will also be aware of diminishing returns and flat areas. Familiarize yourself with how the client reports earnings because each company has its own unique way of presenting the information to the public or its employees.

You are probably asking yourself why you would bother tracking financial earnings of a company you are doing business with, or even one that is not yet a client. Believe it or not, financial information gives hints as to the success of the sales force, the marketing efforts, and the leadership of the executives. The financials can paint a picture that says more than what you are being told. If you still do not believe me, read through the next example.

John B. was getting ready to submit a proposal to company Z; he had some solid ideas about their marketing and sales strategies that would lead to further revenue generation. He checked the financials for the last six quarters and saw that they had very limited growth. He thought this strange as the products they sold were in great demand and they were running at capacity. As he started to dig further into the story, he found that they did not want to grow any more and were content with the status quo. The company was in the process of being absorbed by a larger firm and the CEO was ready to retire. If John had not used his power page appropriately, he might have sent a premature proposal that would have been a waste of time for himself and his customer.

Even though this is a sad story for John, he confirmed the value of doing his research on the financials. He now looks at these before writing a proposal for improvement. What we sometimes view as pain is not pain at all but is simply some other issue at work behind the scenes.

101. Account Plan

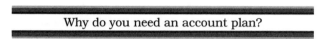

Why do you need an account plan?

When you first decide to approach a company through an introduction, networking event, or as part of your daily routine, you will need to put together an account plan. This account plan will be part of your power page and it will contain information about your own personal approach to winning the account and a plan on when to follow up. Creating an account plan is like setting goals. You have the ultimate target and the steps to get where you ultimately want to be. One thing about the account plan is that sometimes it takes a long time to get from where you are now to where you want to be, in regards to the company you are approaching; sometimes we never get there!

I once put an account plan together and my target was a large corporation that shall remain nameless. The elapsed time between beginning the plan and actually fulfilling the plan was three years. I had to jump through a lot of hoops in order to get to the right people. The timing was also crucial: I had to gauge the best time of the budget year to approach the company, and also make sure I had the right knowledge to get in the door. In another case, I put a plan together for another large corporation, found a contact whom I already knew from fundraising events, and picked up the contract in fourteen days. I basically knew where I wanted to go with the account and followed through.

Planning and goal setting can be onerous for most of us. It is especially difficult to set company and personal goals, but it is extremely important to do them without fail. The only time I have really succeeded in gaining accounts is when I planned the process.

102. *Account Meeting Agenda*

How should you keep track of meetings?

Have you ever wanted to run away from a meeting? I worked for one of the top five companies in the United States and they seemed to *hold* meetings to *plan* meetings. It absolutely drove me around the bend! I would try and multitask like all the other participants and hoped they would not call on me for any information. In the long run, I did not get any value out of these meetings and my work was being ignored. I had to keep track of the meetings and place action items in my calendar so I would remember what the heck it was they wanted. In simple terms, my attitude absolutely stank!

When it was my turn to run the meeting, I decided to make changes. I planned what we should discuss and not just get updates from everyone. The meeting changed from keeping us up to date to one with meaning and relevant issues. Once this change happened, there was more of a necessity to record the minutes and track the meeting progress. Meetings are a crucial part of running a company and winning clients. Client meetings should run smoothly and not be time wasters. You need to get to the point and move on.

Keeping track of meetings and agendas only required the use of tables in a word processing program or the use of an Excel spreadsheet. This allowed the use of check marks to identify those action items that were completed. A list of issues yet to be resolved was easy to spot and did not require retyping everything. Action items for customers should be tracked in the same simple manner. Customers expect to have their items taken care of ASAP. If you do not take the time to record the information, you will not likely remember what they wanted.

The aim of this process is to service the customer and to keep you on track. Milestones, action items, and other events will likely keep you busy. Do not fall down on the job and forget what it is you were supposed to do.

103. *Business Review*

What is the satisfaction and expectation
review of the business history to date?

You have spent a lot of time and effort gathering information about your clients and potential customers. You have kept track of everything that you need to know and have followed up with precision. It has now been a while since you have updated any financial information as you find that you do not have the time—or in reality do not want to find the time. If you have been working according to your action plan, the work should be quite easy. All you want to do in the review process is to go back over your account plan and place an update as to your progress. This progress report to yourself will lead you to further action with the account. This is not a sales course but simply a way to stay connected with those whom you have met. It is the touch points that keep your name in front of the client or potential client.

Using your power page to keep you on track, you perform a business review that will help you to decide whether the business is worth pursuing. Sometimes the path will seem too long to complete, but that alone should not be the reason for dumping the contact. You should look at your financial analysis, possibilities for projects, dollar values if you win the job, expertise required. Once you have reviewed all the information, you should decide which projects you still want and which you should eliminate. By the way, you should always look for new business and shed some of the old that no longer fits into your value proposition. The reason is that you are growing, and old methodologies soon fall away and are replaced by new ones.

Reviewing where you are should not be left to the end of the quarter. You should think about your progress at the end of every month. It does not take a great deal of time for a quick review if you have kept your power page information up to date.

104. Current Initiatives

How do you plan and implement a
work in progress for existing projects?

Another place to do more planning! I believe that if you spend the time planning and do it well, you will have to spend very little time doing the actual work. For example, when writing a book, I spend hours planning the chapters that I want to include. I also spend time outlining topics within those chapters and finally the keywords that belong with the topic. I spend time brainstorming with others and throwing out ideas that do not work. Once this is accomplished, I research the topics, and then I set to the task of writing. Without the planning, the book would be scattered and not well organized.

If you approach your planning with the same discipline (you may want to define your own process for doing so) you will find that the actual work will flow much more smoothly. You will have notes all along the way on the discussions of the deal and also from meetings. You will also have a record of when to follow up and what it is that the client may want to know. Plans should be made for every current initiative that includes a follow-up plan.

Your action plan for your current projects will need to be updated daily. Call this a synopsis of what you have accomplished for each client. Daily updating also makes it easier at reporting time as you will have a record of everything that happened every day.

105. *Future Plans*

How to identify future solutions and opportunities?

Your power page, if used extensively, will help you to identify areas where the client may need more help or may need to purchase additional products. When you read through your notes, you will be able to pinpoint areas that will be a business pain. Customers are always happy to find solutions to potential problems if they see their value. But you must do your homework on various solutions before you make any suggestions. It is too easy to just promote your own company and its products. Make sure you know how the competition fits into the picture and what they can also offer to solve that same problem.

Your power page should also contain competitor information. You need to know what others are doing in the marketplace and what their perceived value is to your client. You need to be better informed and better prepared than anyone else. You want to make it easy for the client to choose you over others. Tighten your business relationship by following through with promises and providing value. Your power page should contain all the information you need to keep the customer.

Checklists

What items do you like to keep track of during visits to clients?

_____

_____

_____

Choose one potential client and fill in the information plan for that company. (see section 92 for the information plan):

Contact information:

_____

_____

_____

Sales Volume:

_____

_____

_____

Problems the company is encountering:

_____

_____

_____

Who are their customers and what is their opinion of the target company?

_____

_____

_____

For your lead contact, list all of the personal information you can gather (birthdates, anniversary, hobbies, other interests, club memberships, etc.):

_____

_____

_____

_____

List 2 or 3 pieces of business you have recently lost and the reason(s) why you lost the deal (be honest with yourself!):

_____

_____

_____

_____

What things can you do for the "lost" customer in order to keep in touch so that you may be considered when new business or projects are on the horizon?

_____

_____

_____

_____

What is your VALUE proposition? What do you bring to the table for your customers? How have you verified your value?

_____

_____

_____

8. Business Card Marketing

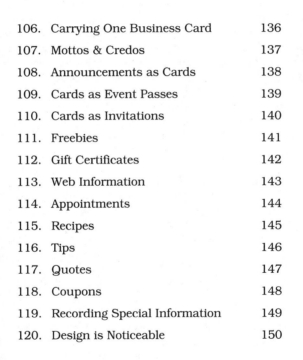

106. *Carrying One Business Card*

> If you are worried about how many different
> business cards you should carry, let me speak
> from experience: You need only ONE!

The best way to confuse a potential customer is to present him with more than one business card. You may be doing a number of things and have a card for each one (even for several companies where you do work), but you need to focus on what you do best. I remember being at a Chamber mixer talking to a man who wanted me to come by his shop to have my logo redesigned. I was handed his business card with a great design and was impressed. I told him that I was currently updating my Web site and should also have my logo updated. At that point he handed me another card and said he did Web site design and wrote content. Now I was totally confused! I needed a graphic designer and not someone who did everything for me. I do not believe that a good graphic designer would want to do websites as that skill is more than making pretty pictures. It would require extensive programming knowledge plus database design, security information, and server expertise. He then handed me another card with "programmer" on it.

I made my decision to go elsewhere as he had become a chameleon in front of my eyes, just grabbing for any business that would come his way. You need to stick to one business card that represents everything that you do. Your card is what you focus on; anything else can be left to a later discussion if it fits in with your business model. It is not difficult to create one business card that has a focus, particularly if you work for a large organization, but if you work on your own, you need to know what your expertise really is.

Your card should clearly identify you and your business and give people your contact information. You may also want to have a title that encompasses your expertise. Do not overcrowd the card with too many details, as it is not likely to get read; keep it clean and simple. At the same time, do not put too little information either. Nothing is worse than seeing a card with a company name that gives you no clue as to what the company does, even if it is just consulting. Always include your Web address: That is where all the extra information can be garnered.

107.   *Mottos & Credos*

Company mottos can easily
be printed on a business card.

Sometimes you wonder if a company motto is remembered by any of its employees. If you ask them, they will have to search around to see if they can find where they wrote it before they can tell you. Most often, the motto is so lengthy that it is totally ignored by everyone except the person who wrote it. The best tack for you is to write one that has meaning and that you can recite easily to your customers. I have a friend who is president of Ionics Fidelity Purewater; his motto is printed on a business-size card that he keeps in his wallet. This is given to each employee and, when asked, they can always find it. The motto is fairly short and to the point; it is something that they use all the time.

A motto is only as good as the degree to which it is used and adhered to. Everyone needs to buy into it and commit it to memory. If it makes no sense and is not relevant to the work you are doing, you will not likely remember it. I use my 10-second pitch as my motto and encourage everyone who does work for me to use it when meeting people for the first time. My motto is "to provide corporations with the tools to maintain, repair, and tune up business processes." If someone wants a further explanation, I give my additional 30-second pitch. How does your motto fit into your client introductions?

Mottos and credos are a good way to emphasize the way you want your customer to value your products and services. It is likely the first thing they see on your office wall or even on your printed materials. The important thing to remember is that it must be useful and can be easily recited by everyone who works for you.

108. *Announcements as Cards*

Announcements can be
handed out as a business card.

Announcements can be more than just a press release that lets the world know that something special has occurred at your place of business or to you personally. You can make announcements for almost anything. You can use it to invite people to a seminar, declare a promotion, or even announce the appointment of an executive. However you decide to use announcements does not matter. What does matter is that you do take the time to use them. I remember working with a printing company that was having difficulty understanding how to do PR for itself. They felt that they had to have hired a new manager or gain a huge contract to be newsworthy. They were only sending press releases and announcements to the local papers and even then they did not get printed. They did not create excitement about what they were doing.

When using announcements you must make certain that what you are announcing is of interest to others. There is no point in announcing you have a new dog at the print shop unless you can make it into a good story. The dog may represent a charity that you are sponsoring or perhaps a mascot. You can make any twist you like for the story—and it must be a true story—to make a newsworthy announcement. It is the way you present the information that is the key to having your announcements noticed.

Like anything else, announcements need to have a reader in order to be acknowledged. Without the audience nothing will happen and the printed materials will end up in the garbage can. Excite your audience so that they want to find out more.

109. *Cards as Event Passes*

Why would you use an event pass?

Event passes are often used as giveaways to entice people to attend some event. For example, most time-share companies give away, in addition to other goodies, passes to be used to attend their spiel. Event passes are used extensively; there is no reason why you cannot put your own together and distribute them to your potential customers. For example, I have a partnership with Power Marketing, and last spring I was tasked with putting on an executive breakfast. The breakfast was free to participants, and the talk was not a sales pitch; it was simply passing out information about the "Seven Deadly Sins of Selling" based on a white paper the Power Marketing people wrote (which is available on my Web site, BizMechanix.com). I created event passes using business cards. The card was not necessary for attendance, but I found most people kept it in their wallet because it was the right size.

We gave away 200 passes, which resulted in 117 registrants and 87 attendees. We were very pleased with the results. You can use passes for entrance into a trade show that would normally have an entrance fee attached. Such passes will be deemed much more valuable than the ones I created for Power Marketing. If you want to use the passes as a way for others to get to know you, create an event that you can use for promotion and distribute event passes to your target audience. You will be surprised at the number of people who will attend just because they have tickets!

The key to event passes is that you do not attach a fee to them. If you decide to charge full price, selling your event will be a little more difficult. An alternative is to give the buyer a discount. Whichever way you decide to promote the event, the best is always free. Save yourself time in designing passes by using business cards. Remember, these events are the ones that you create.

110.   *Cards as Invitations*

Business card size works well
for invitations to special events.

What do you visualize when you think about invitations? More than likely you think of a wedding or a party. You may even think about a spoken invitation that is extended to you for a business event. Invitations come in all sizes and shapes and for almost every event. So how can you get your invitation to your business event noticed? Here are three easy steps that may help increase the attendance at your events.

First, network with those that you would like to attend your event and ask them personally about their calendar—if they have some time free and if you can set an appointment with them at the date and time of your event. This will generally yield a yes. Tell them you will phone and remind them a couple of days ahead of time to confirm their attendance. You may then mail a business card invitation at that point so they have a printed reference.

Second, phone everyone you personally know who is relevant to your gaining more business and ask each if he or she would be available on the date and time of the event. Tell those who respond yes why you would like to see them at that specific time. Mail those who agree to attend one of your business card invitations.

Lastly, you will need to invite previous clients. If they cannot attend at the specified date and time, ask if they know of anyone else in their organization who can take their place. If they do, simply book them in and tell them you will send a reminder.

It is quite easy to get the invitations noticed. The most difficult thing is to make sure those agreeing to attend actually do. You will probably find there is a 20% to 30% fall off between the two numbers. If you plan for this fall off, you can determine how many people to invite in order to fill the room.

111. Freebies

Why give freebies?

We have all seen freebies at trade shows and we have all probably seen the person who goes from booth to booth collecting as many of them as possible. There is always someone who goes only to get the free stuff, but people also go to learn about new products or services. These people may be genuinely interested in what you have to say. Even if they are, there must be something in it for them (we call the phenomenon WIFM—pronounced whiffem—What's in it for me?). Perhaps the freebie you offer should be in the form of a free consultation for a limited time, say a half hour. Or you may want to give out special premiums to potential new clients. To do that you first have to weed out those who just want something for nothing from the true potential business prospects.

Instead of giving away freebies at the trade show desk, you could give attendees a business card that can be used to redeem their freebie. This will drive the customer traffic back to where you would like it to be. For example, a car dealership I did some work for went to every trade show in the area. They had great give-away items but found that not many people came back to the dealership for a test drive, which could have led to an eventual purchase. To rectify the problem, they gave out a business card with the event name, identifying the gift to be given, and explaining that in order to claim the gift, you needed to go to the dealership and take a test drive. The gift was a nice set of steak knives in a butcher's block. The result was that 20% of the people attending the show actually went to the dealership and took a test drive, leading to 25 cars being sold—a much better return for their freebies!

Freebies do not need to be expensive steak knife sets; they can simply be pens with your name on them. Whatever you choose, make sure it is something that can be used and not thrown away. Do not pick a silly cheap toy that will break after one or two uses. Gift certificates may work better than freebies.

112.   *Gift Certificates*

How would you use
business cards for gift certificates?

I asked at the beginning of this chapter how many business cards you need and answered that you need only one. Although this is true when you are trying to form business relationships, it is not true when it comes to promoting your business. Promotion can come in many forms, but using business cards to represent a gift certificate will make it easier for your potential customer not to lose it. You can issue gift certificates for a two-for-one dinner, a discount when coming into your store, or for time at the driving range. Whatever it is that you decide to use it for, you will find that usage will climb considerably if they are in a format that can be readily tucked into a wallet. When you go to most grocery stores or retail stores, they sell gift certificates in the form of "credit cards." These are swiped across a reader at the register when a purchase is made and the amount remaining is loaded on the card.

This is a very expensive form of gift certificate for most small businesses. You can use the same principle, but in paper format. Business cards can range in thickness from paper-thin to fairly heavy stock. The heavier the stock, the more likely the card will not be lost.

I once helped a small grocery store promote its business and gain new customers in the neighborhood by having "gift certificates" for a free gallon jug of milk. We decided on a jug because most people do not purchase just a quart if they have a family. This promotion drew in almost everyone in the neighborhood and the store gained new customers through the attention. You do not need to give away the farm, or in this case the cow; you just need to use a format that will work for you. Once a customer is in your store, you can start working on the business relationship.

Your gift certificate, invitation, announcement, or whatever should also contain your Web information.

113.   *Web Information*

Getting people to go to your Web site is not always easy: Remind them with a special business card.

Whether you understand it or not, the Web is likely here to stay; those businesses that do not yet have a Web presence, or at least e-mail addresses, are likely to get left in the dust. All of your correspondence and especially your business card should contain some reference to your Web site. If you have gained their interest, people want to know more about what you do. What better way to tell them about you than through your Web site? We will discuss what to do with websites in a subsequent chapter. Your business card is the key that can open the door to many business relationships and your Web or e-mail address gives people an easy way to contact you. The argument some people give for not publishing an e-mail address is that they will get junk e-mail as a result. I want to emphasize that you may well get some junk e-mail, but for the most part you will get good correspondence.

I attended and had a display at a Chamber symposium this past year and had a bowl for drawing a giveaway. Our prize was a two-day sales process training seminar. We told people that they should not put their card in for the drawing unless they were truly interested in the training. No problem there, for the winner of the drawing was really excited and made sure that he had all the information he needed in order to attend. At home that evening I went online to register the winner and found that his e-mail address was not printed on his card. I had to enter my e-mail address in order to complete the registration. As a result, he did not get any of the automatic e-mail confirmations. His reasoning was he would get too much junk mail if he placed his e-mail address on a card.

By the way, he ended up sending his partner to the seminar, who saw no problem in giving out his e-mail address. The one thing to remember is you need to specify the ground rules for sending you e-mail.

114. *Appointments*

Doctors do it, hairdressers do it,
and salespeople can do it too.

I have been working with a chiropractor for a few months and when it came time to give me a new appointment, she would use a quarter sheet of paper to check off the appointment time. Inevitably the paper would get lost and not be found when I got home. I suggested to her that she use her business card for a reminder. The patient could write the time and date on the card and then tuck it into her wallet. This method worked so well that the quarter-sheets of paper are now gone. Professional offices use this method sporadically but it certainly makes life easier for the patient. When I set an appointment with a potential customer at a networking meeting, I too use appointment cards. They are printed on only one side with my name, e-mail address, and phone number at the top and a place for the date/time and location of the meeting. There is even room for putting notes or comments. This way I can fill out one for myself and one for my potential customer. The appointment will now be easier to track once I get back to my main calendar.

Your client will also have an easier time remembering when the appointment was set for, and will also have a point of contact if a change needs to be made. It is just another way of making it easy. You can order this type of business card at very little expense if you use a one-color format. Many online printers offer inexpensive cards, but you can also print your own appointment cards yourself using card stock from an office supply store and your word processing program. I would not recommend that you print your own business cards, as you want those to look very professional.

When making appointment cards, you can be quite creative. Just make sure the information you want the client to have is clear. Do not confuse them with unnecessary details.

115.   *Recipes*

Special event and a special recipe:
hand it out on a business card.

Food and good cooking are always of interest to everyone. I have seen many real estate people give out recipes with their newsletter. I find one typed onto a full sheet almost every month. Some of the recipes look absolutely delicious, but I find that the extra information and consequent size of the sheet make it not worth keeping (at least for me). A way of getting your recipes in the hands of the consumer is to put them on something that is easy to store in a recipe box or keep under a magnet on the fridge. If the recipe will fit on a business card, you can slip it in with the newsletter you distribute. The drawback to using a business card is that the recipe cannot be long and complicated. Send them to your Web site for further details and more information!

Entice prospective clients with a few good recipes and tell them where to get more; this will help you build your contact list. Get them to join your mailing list to find out when a new recipe is added. Make sure that you have your Web site and e-mail address on the cards so they can contact you for further information. I once sent out a post card with a recipe everyone kept asking for over the years. I simply sent out a picture postcard with the finished dish on the front and a short note telling them where to find the recipe on my Web site. Although I no longer have this recipe on my site, people kept the cards and actually went online for years afterwards.

Food may be a way to the customer's stomach but there are other uses for business cards that will yield more contacts for your database. Everyone, for example, wants to know time-saving tips.

116. Tips

> The best way for someone to
> hang onto a tip is on a business card.

Do you remember seeing the TV commercials for OSH Hardware stores in which they give out time-saving tips on remedying things like squeaky floors and a host of other common household problems? The tips are well received and they are getting their name associated with their slogan, "The answers are out there." Of course, it's not easy to really take advantage of a tip on the TV. It would be more practical to write it down and stick it in a location where you can easily access it, perhaps even in a folder on your computer.

In the same fashion, you can print your own tips on a set of business cards that contain one tip per card. You can give out the cards at intervals and keep coming up with more over a period of time. If the tips are of value to clients, they will likely collect them for future use. Once again, you will need to place your Web site and e-mail address on the cards so that you are identified with the promotional item.

Tips allow you to share your knowledge and help your customers. If you can make things easier for them to understand or give them a shortcut that helps save time and money, you will be a hero. Heroes are always called upon to solve other problems as well. The important thing is that tip cards are another way for you to gain a touch point with your client or potential client. Take some time to think of what you know that can be easily shared to save your client time and money. But think of quick tips, not a knowledge dump.

Although tips work well, you still need to distinguish yourself. You can do this by thinking of unusual things that are not common knowledge and that will give your customer an advantage. Be creative.

117. *Quotes*

Famous quotes that keep you thinking.

Have you ever heard a speaker say something that you want to make note of and use later? More than likely, you will write it down and file it away, never to be uttered again. The saying could be motivational or it can be something that changes your attitude about your work. If you can capture some of these sayings, you could refer to them often. You can then share these with clients and use them for promoting your business. If you look on the Web, you will find that some printers have a series of motivational sayings placed on business cards and all you need to do is add your personal information to the back of the card.

If you are the one giving the speech and you use sayings that you think will capture the audience's imagination, think about having them printed on a business card. You may find that you will have a "set" of these sayings that you can sell or use as giveaways. Take a look around you and see what sayings belong to you—do not infringe on anyone's copyright or you may find yourself employing a lawyer.

Quotes can be used from other people providing you get permission and give them a byline or they are in the public domain. Just make sure that what you print is perfectly legal.

118. *Coupons*

Turn a coupon into a business card (or vice versa).

Coupons are seen everywhere: You clip them from the newspaper to save on groceries, you get them in the mail to save on brand name items, you even get packages in the form of booklets delivered to your door. Almost everyone believes in doing coupons. I always look to see if a restaurant I love is having a promotion and if my favorite ice cream is on sale at the grocery store, and I imagine that most people are the same. Some people even have a filing system for coupons and make a hobby of collecting them and making money in the process. I am not suggesting you go that far, but you can use a business card for a coupon.

If you want a customer to purchase your product for the first time and you happen to know she is already interested, offer her a coupon on her first purchase. Retailers that want new customers for their credit cards do the same thing. Once customers have the card in their hands, they are more likely to spend at the store. The same is true for any business that wants new customers and also wants to form new business relationships. Hand them a discount coupon for either your products or services, or you can make arrangements with a local restaurant to purchase coupons that you hand out for a free meal.

Coupons are an excellent additional way to keep a business relationship alive. When I worked in a marketing department, my favorite thing was when our suppliers gave us tickets or coupons for special events.

119. *Recording Special Information*

Use a business card as a note pad
for recording important information.

I am sometimes asked why I make such use of business cards. My reply is that they are easy to transport and do not require an extra envelope. I particularly make use of others' business cards for taking notes on our conversation. I am one of the worst, when I get home, at remembering who Gary from XYZ is and what he does that will make a good connection. Write it down right after the conversation; make the notes very brief, but make sure that you write down why you are interested in furthering the relationship. You do not need a lot of lines of information, but you do need to note when you agreed to contact that person and why. The other person is not likely to remember who you are either, and if you have a few notes, he will appreciate it as well when you contact him.

Special information is only special if it leads to a business relationship and ultimately to doing business with that person. Make sure you know exactly what you expect to get out of the contact. Do not bother contacting everyone you meet—if you do, you will not have time to get down to the real business of making money. I only write down information for those that I put in my "interested" list so that I can follow up with a brief meeting to explore the possibilities. If I am not in the market for an item or for some reason I do not want to meet with the person, I file the card away in a separate location. I never throw out valuable contact information.

I do have a large database of contacts that I add to every day. I also make note, in my contact file, of what potential there is or what service that person could possibly need from me or my company. Not everyone will be a buyer, but everyone knows someone who may be one.

120. *Design is Noticeable*

You need only one card, but make it noticeable.
Make sure it says the right thing.

I mentioned before that you can make some cards using your computer. However, I would suggest that you take the time and expense to have them designed in order to look professional. A good designer will cost at the beginning of the process, but, over time, the cost will be negligible compared to the amount of business you can generate by simply using a business card. Your main card should have a simple and clear design that makes it easy for the recipients to contact you. The card should indicate what type of business you are in as well. I have seen so many business cards that leave me wondering what the person or the company does. For example, at a fund-raising meeting for a Chamber in my local area I was given a set of business cards for contacting possible suppliers of goods for the event. More than half the cards bore only inscriptions like "Tecon Incorporated." I had no idea what these outfits did or what they could possibly supply. As a result, I called only on those companies that clearly defined what they sold.

Take a look at your own business card. Does it spell out clearly what you do? If someone picked up your card because you left it at a potential client's office, would the person be able to figure out what you do? Would he or she even read the card?

If your business card is well designed and presents a clear message, you will be portrayed with a professional image. Displaying your Web site address and your e-mail contact information will give a potential client another way to contact you. All other components of your business stationery and Web site should also be well designed. The message you give your customers should be consistent.

Checklists

How many business cards do you have? _____

Of all your business cards, which one business brings you the most income?

_____

_____

What is your company motto (not your mission statement)?

_____

_____

_____

_____

What event or product could you announce using a business card?

_____

_____

_____

_____

If your company has give-aways, what are they and why would a potential business partner want to have any of them?

_____

_____

_____

_____

If you were to use appointment cards, what information would you put on that card as a reminder for your customers?

_____

_____

_____

_____

What special tips can you give to your potential clients that will help them make a decision to use your company next time they have a problem in your area?

_____

_____

_____

_____

Using your imagination, what other things can you print on a business card that will help ensure your card will be kept on hand?

_____

_____

_____

_____

_____

_____

_____

_____

9. Web Relationships

121. *The Web*

How can you be found on the Web?

The Web is a necessity, as everyone knows by now. You will be asked about your Web site in almost every meeting with clients. You may also be asked about it at any of the networking groups you attend. Why do people ask? Simply to verify what you are saying. The Web has a tendency to substantiate all of the elevator pitches and spiels that you give when first meeting people. When I first started out reinventing myself and wishing to go back to my consulting background, I called on someone whom I had worked with on some interesting projects. I told her what I was planning on doing, since the project we were working on was canceled. I forwarded my contact information outside of the project and the first thing she did was to look at the Web site I had at that time (www.BizMechanix.com). Although this site is not my main one, it gave her enough information about my expertise. I did not have to mail out brochures, send my resume, or spend time explaining my background. All of my information was available on the Web and was downloadable as a PDF file. This goes without saying (but I'll say it anyway): Do not put anything on your Web site you do not want the public to see.

One of the things that we did was to make sure that we had keywords and a descriptor on the site. This enabled us to register with search engines (the places that have information about your Web site when people search for you, so your page will come up in the search results). Search engines also found the site when my name was entered. I was actually quite surprised at all the pages my name was on. Type your name into a search engine such as Google and see what you get. If you do not appear, take some time to figure out why and do something about it. The easier you make it for clients and potential clients to find your site, the greater the opportunity is for you.

A Web site is like an electronic brochure; it describes your business and also describes all of the things that you can do to solve problems. A Web site is an important tool and you should learn how to use it.

122. *Downplay Sales Pitch*

When building a relationship,
listening is more important than talking.

A Web site can reveal a great deal about your business, even answer questions about whom you have done work for in the past. It is a great place to put testimonials and quotes from current and past customers. The Web is also a good place to sell your products or services. There have been many articles about how the Web has yielded a disappointing number of sales as compared to regular sales venues such as a retail location. Although this may be true, the Web is still an excellent forum for putting in your sales pitch in a manner that the customer can better understand. To promote yourself, you can toot your own horn and explain what a good job you are doing and still look extremely professional.

In your promotion, make sure the customer can cut through the extraneous materials and get to the heart of the matter. I hate going to websites that spend their whole time giving me hype and a giant sales pitch. I usually go to a site to get more information about a company, see who the players are, what kind of business they do, where they are located, and how they can help my business. If a site is obviously only there to pitch me, I usually go on to the next company that gives me the information I want. People go to sites for information and advice; they will not read the hype. Put your support materials online and drive them to the site.

Flashy may be good for some websites but when you are doing business, you need to get to the point. Give out information freely— do not expect anyone to add an e-mail address to your list before you give something out. Otherwise, more often than not they will go elsewhere.

123. *Alliances on the Web*

Be picky about who will link to you;
shoot and scatter does not always work.

Having a Web site is not enough by itself to get you noticed. You will need to do a number of things to have your site become better known. Here are three ideas that you may want to use.

First, find another business that is a good fit for what you do and have your information displayed on their site; you will probably also need to display their information on your site. Do not pick just any site for this exchange of information. Make sure the other sites have the same business values as you. I personally do not use other sites unless there is value in it for both parties.

Second, make sure you are active in newsgroups such as Yahoo groups in your area of expertise. Newsgroups are not a place to tout your business, but they are a place to give free advice and get yourself known in the process. Just make sure the group you join and the advice you give fits in with your business model.

Third, you will need to have your Web address printed on everything you give out—and I mean everything. The Web address should be on your business cards, letterhead, envelopes, brochures, white papers, articles you write, all your advertising materials, donations, and any business listings. Besides promoting yourself on the Web, you need to promote the Web on everything you do. You want to drive people to the site to learn more about you and what you do. Just make sure you have a separate Web site for each line of business.

Some people sell goods on their sites and join a group such as the Commission Junction. Commission Junction allows you to choose what other products you will sell by placing a banner on your site. You can also place your goods in the listings for others to choose. You will not make a great deal of money this way, but it is an avenue for selling products.

124. *Offering a Free Service*

> Build it and they will come is not always true;
> you have to form a relationship with the company
> before you will get quality attendees
> or participants for a free service.

The old saying is, the way to a man's heart is through his stomach (true? true for a woman too?). True or not, the way to a Web surfer's heart is through free information and products. Simply offering free information is not enough to bring visitors to your site. The offering has to have substance and be worthwhile. The Web surfer is constantly asking, "What's in it for me?" If what you are providing is of value, the word will get out fast. Your service can be anything from free training, white papers, advice, or even a newsletter. Even though you have the information available, you must still inform everyone you know that it is in place.

My husband does a lot of volunteer work for Rotary and is the district webmaster. He has placed hundreds of pages of information on this site, offering the various clubs tools they can use. Although some make extensive use, others have difficulty understanding why they would go there. He spends a great deal of his time showing the value of the site. He even posted free e-learning components on the site so that visitors could learn how to use an application. It takes work to show people the value of the site.

Eventually, over a period of a couple of years, the Web site came to be used by almost every club. Now they are submitting information about events so that their clubs are part of the process. You should look at your site in the same way. It is a tool for your customers to access free information, and the more valuable you make that information, the more often they will look on the Web. If your free information is only hype, they will turn away in droves.

Although you do not want to overwhelm anyone with information, you can make your site very informative. Make it easy to navigate so visitors can find what they want. If you have more information to give out than can be professionally displayed, consider putting out a newsletter on current events and other newsworthy items.

125. *Newsletter Frenzy*

Offer a newsletter in a time frame
that will be easy for you to manage.

Although doing a newsletter is a great idea, do not be too quick to jump on the bandwagon. Almost everyone is doing it, but not all are doing it well. The newsletter with the greatest frequency can get quite annoying for the recipients unless it is packed full of useful information. Only those who have a relationship with your company will continue to subscribe.

Even though you may have great information to give away, you must also consider the time it takes to put a good newsletter together. If you are doing a daily, you will need to spend at least 3 hours putting it together and another few hours editing, polishing, and answering queries. If, on the other hand, you decide weekly is good, you will still need to spend those 3 hours and then some, but now it will be once a week. You also need to determine what day of the week to distribute the newsletter. Some times are better for getting read than others. You may want to do some research to find out when is the best time to deliver to your intended audience.

If you do a monthly, you are more like an e-zine. You will be expected to have more than just a few great articles; you will need to add graphics and images to enhance what you have to say. You will also need to research the background of submissions from other people. A monthly sometimes makes it easier to ask for submissions, but you do have to make sure the articles fit with your business principles. A monthly can often take more work than anticipated; you will likely want to have everything in hand to publish at least three months in advance.

Doing a newsletter requires a commitment of time and effort. If you promise to deliver at a certain time each day or week or month, you will need to deliver on time. Not doing so will jeopardize your credibility. A way around this might be to produce white papers.

126. White Paper Downloads

People like white papers that offer value.
Expound on your expertise and make
yourself the master of the subject.

As we mentioned, newsletters take a great deal of effort and require schedules, time lines, and other milestones that must be met precisely. If you think that these demands are too much for you, consider writing a white paper or two. A white paper is an informational essay that spans from two to a maximum of 10 pages. The white paper is not a forum for advertising your company or its products. It is, however, a forum for displaying your expertise and giving free advice. A white paper gives your audience the opportunity to learn something from you without fear of follow-up phone calls and without an outright display of the sales pitch.

A company that I work for has such a white paper, entitled "The Seven Deadly Sins of Selling." This paper gives information only on the sins and why they are detrimental to you. It has been downloaded thousands of times and has generated numerous queries for more information about the training programs that are associated with the sales process. You can download this and other white papers from my site, BizMechanix.com, or from PowerMarketingWorld.com.

What expertise do you have to offer that can be put into a white paper? What advice can you give? Simply use a format for the information such as the ones on my site. White papers will help to establish you as the expert in your market. When your expertise is in writing and can be distributed freely, people find it easier to contact you for more information. You can take the white paper further by offering a seminar under the same topic.

127. *Event Registration*

Creating a smooth event registration system for
events is crucial for keeping customers.

If you have ever put on an event, you know that registration can be
very tiring and cumbersome. If it is a large event, you will have a
computer system that takes care of the registrations. The Web can
also be used for registration just as it can be used to have people
register for your newsletter. Event registration on the Web enables
you to drive people to your site and then navigate to the registration
page. This way they get a taste of who you are and what you do at
the same time that they are registering. Unfortunately, not everyone
will register from the Web site and you will still need to enter some
names by hand. This is not a big task if your anticipated audience is
fairly small, but for a larger event you will need to deal with the
process differently. Services such as Aceteva.com make the process
very simple.

When I was setting up the executive breakfast for my Power
Marketing seminar, I had people go to the Power Marketing Web site
to register. It was the only option they had. I found that a number of
people wanted to register but were not computer savvy enough to
navigate the process. I contacted them by e-mail and asked for their
information and entered it into the registration form on their behalf.
Only a handful of people did not want to do this for themselves.

In the long run, you can also have people pay for events on the Web
at the same time. If you do not have the ability to take credit cards
over the Web, you can use a payment service such as PayPal. It will
take the orders and process the credit cards and even deposit the
monies into your bank account.

128. Tips & FAQs

> Offer the manual and special tips
> to enhance the customers' experience.

How much is spent, by yourself or your customer, on user manuals for your products? How often do your customers call you with routine questions that could be answered through the user manual? The answer to these questions may vary, but an easy way to give your customers all the information they need is to provide the user guides online. These online guides will enable free lookup without tying up valuable phone lines and sales time for you. Although contact with the customer is ideal, often you will get bogged down on giving out too much help when the information is right in the guide.

If you provide the information on the Web, you will get fewer calls and the calls you do get will be more technical in nature. This way you will be able to better service your customers with more difficult problems. You will also not be wasting their time in looking up information that is generally called routine. I am not saying you want to discourage customers from calling; you just want to cut down on the calls that can be handled by a frequently asked questions (FAQ) page on your site or a Web version of the user guide.

Customers are always grateful for easy-to-find and -understand information, and if you provide online guides, you should also consider putting up or retaining guides for older models of your products. People actually keep products and make use of them many years after later models have arrived. They will also call you for help in replacing parts or simply maintaining them. Be of service to the customer, and keep the business relationship going.

129. *Opt-In Email Lists for Events*

Ensure that your mailing list has
actually agreed to accept your newsletter.

Opt-in lists for events are similar to the signing up for a newsletter. You ask people if they want to be notified when a special event or sale is happening. Although some may look at this as a permission to send junk mail, you can let them know that you are not selling your list to anyone and you will use it only for the stated purpose. Then do not abuse the privilege of having them sign up. Do not overwhelm them with sales and event notices—make sure that you schedule the notices and let them know when to expect them. As with a newsletter, you can tell them whether it will be daily, weekly, monthly, or otherwise. You should also inform them of the day to expect it.

I know that you do not commonly see much scheduling happening on the Web in general, but you will find that your clients appreciate your scheduling. It gives them a heads up when to expect the information so they are more likely to read it. You want them to read it and take action from what you send. In order to make this happen, schedule your mailings and make them exciting and enticing.

If people opt in, they will also want to have the option of opting out. Let them know at any time they can do so and give them a link so they can follow through. I have opted out of some lists with ease and others only with great difficulty. As you can imagine, I feel respect for the companies that make it easy and lose all patience for those that do not. Consider, too, that people change addresses, and they must have an easy way to opt out of the old address and opt in with the new one!

130. E-Books

> Offer an e-book only if it is part of
> a training program, not replacing print.

Have you ever read an e-book or at least had a chapter or two sent to you to read? If you are like most people, you ended up printing the book and reading it that way. E-books have commonly been treated like normal books that contain pages of text with few illustrations. If you are going to produce an e-book, you need to discover the power of using the Web. You can do many creative things with HTML and graphics to produce a book that comes alive on the screen. Do let yourself be talked into writing the book, text format, and then reproducing it for the Web in long columns of text. Make sure you have the use of photos or pictures to liven up the images you paint with your words.

You can make the book truly interactive. You can use interactive checklists that produce a list of tasks for readers. You can ask them to fill in forms, and make decisions that lead them to another location in the materials. The book should also contain links to references so that the reader can learn more than what you are telling them. The possibilities are endless. If you are going to produce an e-book, use your imagination and make the book an experience the reader will want to repeat and tell others about.

Reader involvement not only reinforces what you are saying, it gives them the opportunity to grasp materials. Learning by doing stays longer than just reading the material and putting the book on the shelf. Get your audience involved with your story.

131. Web Contributions

> Your site is not the only place to post
> your expert opinions. Look to other sites too.

Your site is most important to you, but it is also important that you extend your reach beyond your own site and contribute elsewhere. By contribute, I mean writing articles that others can post, joining newsgroups and adding your comments, writing rebuttals for other newsletters and articles. You want to spread out so that your name and expertise become recognized. If you do things only on your own site, you will remain famous on your site alone. Unless you market yourself to others in unobtrusive ways, you will never be recognized as an expert in your field.

You can send out press releases to e-newsletters and e-zines in the same way you do for print materials. Just as you need to follow up with your press releases in print media, you need to do the same within the Web. Locating the contact information for the editors of eMedia may be just a bit more difficult, and the mode of communication often is through e-mail. But if you just e-mail the question, "Did you get my press release?" you may be ignored. On the other hand, if you are able to find the phone number of the individual, you may find that a phone call will get you a lot farther and you may find your release published.

Even better, you may find that you get an interview. eMedia is often better distributed than print media. Having your name and touting your expertise in front of subscribers is just what you need to do to increase your chances of getting more business.

Send out a few test rebuttals to articles and see if you get printed. You should also parallel your efforts with the print media. You can make announcements for others to read about you in a specific Web e-zine.

132. Get Them Hooked

People want experts: Toot your horn
and hook them on what you have to say.

Most experts like to share their knowledge with others. Experts will give advice freely (though they will not give away the farm in the process). If you want to be recognized as an expert, the more information—that is, useful information—you provide, the more people will come back to your Web site. You need to have a hook that has them coming back for more. Ask them what they want, ask for feedback, and then follow up on the feedback. Let them know you are listening to what they have to say. Print their rebuttals in your next newsletter. Have them use your blog. Always respond and keep the information up to date. They will tell everyone they know that they were published on your site.

Keep them coming back by having your audience contribute to your newsletter. Every time you send out a message that you are looking for articles, providing you ask in the correct forums, you will get a good response. Join newsgroups that have writers and let them know that you are putting together electronic information and want to have contributions on a specific subject. You may opt to pay or not to pay for the publishing, depending on your focus. You will not be disappointed with the response.

After all, you can either do all the writing yourself, or you can lessen your load by having other writers. Take a look at the writers' market. They have listings of all kinds of eMedia that are looking for articles. Get your company listed in their directory. If you offer pay, your response will be higher than if you do not.

Get people interested in what they read, and give them a place to send rebuttals and to contribute to your newsletters, and so on.

133. Follow-Up with Web Entries

Keep entries and comments
on other sites up to date.

If you have spent the time and effort to place entries and comments in newsgroups and on other sites, you need a way to track when you placed the information. As you are probably quite aware, information can become dated very quickly, and once your data and information is posted for longer than a week, it is considered old news no matter how valuable you think it is. You must keep on top of the entries and keep them fresh. You do not want to be in the situation where you are at the bottom of the list and people are reading responses from your competitors. Here are three steps to help you avoid that situation.

First, when placing an entry, record into a spreadsheet—Excel, for example—such information as the URL (site address), the date of the entry, the title, and the comment you made.

Second, you will need to sort your list daily or weekly by the date. Make sure the oldest entry floats to the top of the list. Then go to the link that you have placed in the spreadsheet and see where you can add other information or simply update your entry. The update does not have to be lengthy; you may only want to change a few words or a date.

Third, once you have updated the information or added another piece of content, update your spreadsheet with a new date and the changes you made. Always make sure you know what you have on everyone's site!

Following up shows that you have the expertise stated. It also shows that you have a genuine interest in what is happening with the newsgroup. When you are updating, do not advertise your services! Only give out more advice and a way to contact you.

134. Ordering Online

> Make sure you know whom you are
> buying from or you will often bring junk e-mail.

Let's switch roles. You are now the customer and you want to buy something from your site. You know that the items you buy will be shipped to you and arrive in a few days, so there is no instant gratification involved when ordering over the net. Take a look at how easy it is to navigate around your site and how easy is it to get to the place where you can purchase the items. If you find it difficult to get to the online store, make note of it and make some changes. The easier it is to find the items, the easier it is to buy from you.

I am working with a customer that has a great looking Web site, but the navigation and scrolling to purchase are extremely difficult. Some of the links do not work and you cannot get back to the home page. If they made it easier (and we have given them a proposal on how to do that), they would likely increase their sales.

Besides ease of use, you also need to look at the security of the site when doing the purchasing. I would never give my credit card number to a site that does not have a secure server to process the payments. You can tell if it is secure by the lock that is closed at the bottom-right of the screen. If the lock does not appear, I go elsewhere to purchase. One more thing to be aware of is the follow-up you do after the purchase is made.

Most online stores such as Amazon send an e-mail to confirm your purchase. This gives the customer an opportunity to change her mind or refute the purchase. Amazon also sends an e-mail to say that the item has been shipped and when I can expect it at my front door.

Take care and make it easy for your customers. They want to know how much their purchases cost, when the package is to be expected, what additional costs will be incurred by the shipping method chosen, and the total cost of the transaction. They expect you to follow up the order to make sure that they get what they expect and that the goods they ordered are received in good condition.

135. *Drive 'Em to the Site*

> Take every opportunity to send people to your site
> and make sure that there is something in it for
> them; otherwise they will soon fly away.

Now that you have a top-notch professional site with an e-commerce secure store, you are ready to go into business on the Web. You will need to promote your site as you would any new product or service. You will want to put together a public relations campaign such as a professional e-mail message that contains graphics and links. You will need to send the e-mail to all your current customers plus friends and acquaintances. Send it only to people who know you. At this time also prepare a press release announcing your new site and what is special about it. This press release should also be sent to eMedia, as we discussed before.

Your print materials should contain the Web address and a generic (or your own) e-mail. If you spend money on newspaper advertising, you will need to place your Web site address and perhaps an e-mail address. I always include my e-mail address because I want people to e-mail me to ask questions no matter where they saw the ad. I use a generic e-mail address such as info@BizMechanix.com so it does not interfere with my regular e-mail. If you sponsor an event or give a donation, you need to make sure your Web information is on the donation or is part of your sponsorship byline: Do not be shy, put it EVERYWHERE!

Now that we have seen a number of ways to use the Web for our marketing, you must also note that the Web is a good way for potential clients to learn more about you. Before a business relationship can be formed, three things are needed:

First is chemistry. Chemistry simply means that you like the person and find you can get along with him.

Second is integrity. Integrity is discovered through backing up what you say with real-life examples and giving references to your work. If you hesitate, then a business relationship is not likely to ensue.

Last, there must be an appropriate business fit. If there is no match for the two companies, there is no point in pursuing the relationship. The Web will help you discover more about the other company and they will find out more about you in the same way.

Checklists

What message are you giving on your Web site? (Is it the same message you give when you talk to potential business partners?)

_____

_____

_____

_____

What does your Web site provide in order to gather customer feedback?

_____

_____

_____

_____

List the companies that you are affiliated with—and mark those that you have listed or whose logo you have placed on your site.

_____

_____

_____

_____

What free service or products can businesses obtain from your site?

_____

_____

_____

_____

If you have a newsletter, what is its focus?

_____

_____

_____

_____

What tips and FAQs do you have on your Web site?

_____

_____

_____

_____

Does your company have a blog? _____

What types of discussions do you feel would be good for your company blog?

_____

_____

_____

_____

List as many reasons as you can as to why a customer or potential customer would want to return to your Web site.

_____

_____

_____

_____

_____

_____

10. Printed Networking

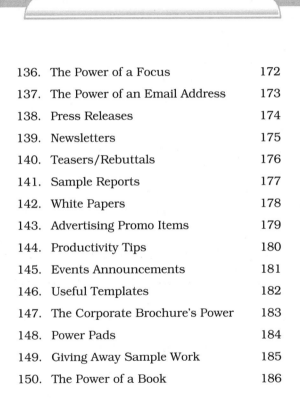

136. *The Power of a Focus*

How do you create focus with a business card?

Focusing on one thing at a time will yield better results when you attend a networking event. Using your business card effectively is the key to being noticed at any event. Most people at an event will be exchanging cards and most cards will be printed in the same fashion. Either they will be white with the logo and contact information, or they will be too busy to read at a glance. Somehow you have to make your card more noticeable than the others.

When I was working exclusively for Power Marketing, I used their card. The card was professionally done with a great logo and design. The card itself caused people to say, "Wow, what a great-looking card!" That alone made me very happy. The back of the card contained more of the design but still allowed the recipient enough space to write comments or notes. I always make first contact after a networking event, and I still got comments about the card: What a lasting impression it made!

Your card is your introduction, and if you look at the way business is done in Japan, the business card is not just a calling card, it is a presentation. They take time to honor your card and honor you as well in doing so. The card is a reflection of who you are. The exchange of cards usually means that the person is interested in doing business with you.

In America we pass out so many cards that we often do not know who has them. I always keep track of who has my card and when he or she received it. Thus, when I change companies or my card is updated, I have a ready-made list of contacts who will receive the new information. It's a great way to increase the number of touch points.

The information on your card is just as important as the card itself. Make sure that any Web information is on the card—your Web site address and an e-mail address. Without it, the card may be tossed! You are after ways to gain business relationships, not cause aggravation.

137. The Power of an Email Address

> Some people will not put their e-mail address on cards that are passed out at a trade show, but if they really want to have you contact them, they do.

Contacting via e-mail is so commonplace today. It is instant contact and instant deletion. The information flows faster than ever when you have an e-mail address. Our company works with a number of clients who exchange all of their information using e-mail. They send images, have company meetings, and even develop training materials all through e-mail. There is little need for face to face; the use of e-mail overcomes long distances.

I keep in constant touch with my children, who live a 16 hour drive away. I basically talk to them every day using chat software and sending emails. I still call them on the phone, but e-mail is so fast that we can leave notes for each other and respond later. The cost is so small as well. Businesses cannot survive and do well if they do not have e-mail to process orders, send information, and get it there on a timely basis.

For example, you will send most press releases today via e-mail. You have an even shorter period of time in which to catch the attention of editors. Some papers, however, still want to have faxes. Email also has its problems. If you sign up for some newsletters, you will end up on mailing lists and get spam mail. I only sign up for companies that say they will not sell the list. I actually use a separate e-mail for newsletters in order to keep my personal e-mail box fairly clean from spam. If you have your own domain (Web address), I suggest you do the same. Use one address for signing up and the other for conducting business.

All of your Web information, such as e-mail address, needs to be on your printed materials. It is a way that potential customers can feel comfortable contacting you. Email is actually far more comfortable than picking up the phone and calling. Sometimes you will send an e-mail and then need to follow up with a phone call. You would do this if you are sending out a press release.

138. *Press Releases*

Press releases allow you to boast about your
expertise and will make you known on the topic.

The first thing to remember about a press release is that you only
have a headline to catch the attention of the journalist or editor. If
that does not make them sit up and take notice, your release is likely
to end up in the wastebasket. You will need to spend time coming up
with unique headlines that get to the point and entice the reader to
move down the page.

The best way to grab headline attention is to read the headlines in
the current paper. What is it that the newspaper prints? You may
find that one thing is of importance to one paper and something
entirely different is to another. What do you do in this case? You
simply change the headline to match the requirements of each paper
you send the release to. It will take a bit of work and research to find
the right fit, but it can be done.

Press releases require the answers to the basic questions such as
who, what, why, when, and where. It has also been said that using
statistics to prove your point is also another attention grabber. If
your headline contains anything to do with money, health, or sex,
you have a better chance of being read. The point is that you need to
work on your headline and pass it in front of others for their reaction
before sending it out.

You also need to make a media list and contact information for the
journalist who reads the headline. And you will need to keep this
media list current, as people in this industry tend to move around
frequently. Press releases can be used for more than just an
announcement. You can tell people about a new product, a new
employee, an award, or anything that is thought to be newsworthy.
Whatever the event you choose to share with the world, do not
overdo it and always follow up.

139. Newsletters

Newsletters will help you
keep in touch with your alumni.

All of us would like to have repeat customers, but by their very nature some of our businesses and services do not lend themselves to repeat customers. For example, one of my clients sells health insurance for only one company. Once you buy, you are not likely to buy from the company again. In that situation the equivalent of the repeat customer is the person who remains a customer for life.

A good way to keep the customer and have repeat business is to provide timely information about your business. The easiest way to do this is to create a newsletter that is sent out at least monthly. A newsletter is a tool for creating awareness about what the customers have purchased and to inform them of new items that are available.

If you go to most websites, they will offer you the option of joining their e-mail list for their newsletter. Joining a newsletter can be a bit of a problem. It is sometimes difficult to tell whether you will be getting information or advertising hype. Take a look at some of the newsletters that are being offered. You should be able to read some of the back issues to get a taste of the format and the usefulness of what they offer.

If you will be printing your newsletter and distributing it via mail, make sure that you are giving out what the market wants. Printing costs can be high, but if you are successful and the newsletter is well received, you can offer both print and electronic versions. Make sure you have the subscription base and the budget to do the mailings. If you send out 65 newsletters each week the costs are very reasonable, but once the letter gets very popular you will need extra income to cover the costs. If not, you should switch to electronic format.

140. Teasers/Rebuttals

> If you read an article and you have the
> expertise, and you either agree or disagree,
> send in a rebuttal or comment; this is
> the easy way to get into print.

Getting your name into print is not as difficult as it first seems. You do not need to write the original article. You can scan newsletters and look for articles in your field, then write a rebuttal or make a comment and send it in to the editors. If they feel you have something valuable to say, they will print your words and credit you, publishing who you are as well (and often also contact information).

Once you have done a few rebuttals and comments on hot topics, your name will be better known and it will be easier to get your articles published in the same paper or magazine. Make sure you can back up what you say. If you cannot back it up, you will do damage to your reputation that you never wanted. It has been said that it takes only one false claim to ruin years of work. Do not put yourself in such a position.

So what type of articles do you want to make comment on? Those that pertain to your business are the best to start. Gain a reputation, let people know who you are, let them know how to contact you. A person who is really excellent at marketing through rebuttals and recognition is Seth Godin. Just type his name into a search engine and see what sites his name is associated with. He has also written a book that is worth reading called *The Purple Cow*, in which he talks about differentiating yourself from the crowd.

With any print materials, you want to make sure that you have the expertise and experience to add to the existing materials. If you want your name to be remembered, comment on everything that pertains to your line of business and get your name known with the editors.

141. Sample Reports

> When people want your advice for free, send
> them a sample of the work you do; you
> will be surprised at the relationships you form.

Virtually everyone in business would like to have services and products for no cost. I work with all kinds of companies, from large to small. Every single one of them wants my information and services for free. I only do pro bono work for nonprofits, and even then, if there is a cost to me I generally try to pass that on. If you give away your time, then you will be valued at that same price.

I visited a client today who wanted help with some aspect of his Web site, and I gladly had my colleague come with me to give some instruction. When we arrived, the person needing help was the same one we had given the information to before. As we did not charge on the first occasion, he had not paid much attention to the process and instructions for how to complete the work. The time spent with him today will be a billable item; I do not like to be taken advantage of in any respect.

A good way to keep such a thing from happening to you is to produce a sample report that gives advice for free. The only cost to you is the printing and the time it takes to write the report. These reports can also be made available on the Web site for downloading. The report can be one or two pages of FAQs (frequently asked questions) or a step-by-step procedure that is common to most industries. The point is to make the information available and free up your time to sell and to do the work that helps you make an income.

The term sample report is often a misnomer. Far too many of them are just come-ons to buy a service. The word free no longer always means free. Many ads in entrepreneurship and start your own business type magazines offer free reports. The problem is that there are really strings attached. For one, you need to send them your address for shipping. If you do that, the junk mail will start. They are more than likely selling the mailing list and making money from the report through advertisers. You need to make a decision to truly offer something for free and respect other people's time. If your materials are good and you do not pester them with other information, they will return to your site for more.

142. *White Papers*

How do you use a white
paper to confirm your expertise?

A white paper is a report that is approximately ten pages in length and that provides valuable information about a topic. It is not hype for a product or service, nor is it a tool for grabbing business. It is simply a place to educate and inform the public about an aspect of your business (and your competitor).

For example, I was working with a company that sold skis and snowboarding equipment in the winter and also sold lacrosse equipment and swimming products. They were in the process of developing their Web site and were trying to find a better way to sell products over the Web. We suggested that they produce a white paper explaining the finer points of selecting the right equipment for each of the sports and also to print these documents for distribution at swap meets and other local events.

The white paper would not advertise any of their products, but they would put the store information on the back of the paper. This way requests for more information could be obtained by contacting them directly. The white paper placed them in front as far as expertise in the industry was concerned, and it was an excellent way to do a soft sell. If you find that you are not able to write such material, use a format similar to the one shown at the end of the chapter and hire a writer to fill in the content. You can then print these for events and also make an electronic version available.

If you have a white paper, you can also put on a seminar based on that paper. A seminar will further establish your expertise. At the seminar hand out your paper plus any newsletters you have produced. Anything you have in printed form will be carried away. Just make sure you have your Web site information and e-mail address on everything.

143. *Advertising Promo Items*

Put your name everywhere—pens, pencils, and notepads: everything potential customers will use— and so keep your name in front of them.

Printed materials do not have to be restricted to newsletters, flyers, white papers, books, and the like. You can create any number of promo items. Pens seem to be a common one. When you think about it, people often feel the need to borrow a pen: Why not give them one with your company name and information on it? And how often have you lent a pen and the borrower kept it, without thinking? You want to encourage this of course.

My daughter once picked up a pen when filling out a form somewhere and inadvertently brought it home. A month later, she was rummaging around for a pen, as she needed to look up a place to buy new insurance. She happened to find that very pen in her junk drawer. Believe it or not, it was for an insurance agency just down the street from where she lived. She called them and ended up buying coverage from them. Although this may be a rare case, it does happen, and pens do act as reminders of what you do.

When you are circulating and networking at events, carry a few extra promo items with you and if you hit a good prospect, offer her one. If the item is a pen, take them everywhere you go—someone is always looking for a pen to write phone numbers and the like. I always hand out a white paper that is relevant to my business when networking and finding a possible client. I want to educate and inform him about what I do without being pushy. Does this work? Yes, but in ways that are not obvious at first. These papers often get handed around at work and then I will get a call. Promo items give enough information to make it easy for potential customers to contact you. Your business name, contact information, and Web address should be printed and easy to read.

The point with a promo item is that you want to be either remembered or noticed. In either case a good promo item will help you achieve this. You can strive to be different, but you are more likely to be noticed if you strive to be useful in everyday business life. Look for things that are unique, useful, and represent you well.

144. Productivity Tips

How can print media help with productivity tips?

I recently received a business card from a person selling local and long distance telephone services. His card held some really useful information. It held tips on how to answer the phone with courtesy. Instead of throwing his card into my deep pile, I pinned it on my wall with the tips facing me. The card is small enough not to interfere with all the other documents I have posted. Using a business card in this manner was an excellent idea; you can expand on this by giving shortcut tips, faster ways to accomplish routine tasks, or even a way to improve processes. I often use job aids for such purposes and really appreciate it when I get some from my suppliers.

Another unique item I received, from a company called Total Rebound: Total Adventures, was a year-long calendar that had a peel off back so I could stick it to the bottom of my monitor. I have seen these in other places too, but it is such a shortcut and time saver for looking up dates, and it provides me a way to increase productivity. Use your imagination to create information that will help your prospects or customers. Use these aids when networking to create a conversation piece, to get people talking.

Giving out pointers, tips, shortcuts, and the like is just another way to catch the attention of potential customers. It gives you (and them) an excuse to talk about what you do. Once the conversation is open, take time to set a first meeting and find out more.

145. *Events Announcements*

> Why make sure that those you know
> do know about your event, and keep
> them informed with printed materials?

Announcing an event can range from being very simple for a small party to being an onerous task for a larger seminar. Each has its method of informing attendees. The first thing that comes to mind for an event is the invitation. I rarely get party invitations through the mail these days, but I do get them by e-mail. The chance of getting my response is actually higher through the use of print media. It seems like I am being treated as a special person when I get a mailed invitation. There are other ways, of course, that you can use print media to gain attention and attract attendees for your events.

If you are offering door prizes or free items to the first one hundred attendees, you are more likely to get a larger audience. In this case, you will want to have not only word-of-mouth advertising but also printed ads in the news media, or events listings in the news calendar page. If you want a large enough audience, you will need to choose a variety of ways to get people's attention. Do not just use e-mail; combine it with print ads and invitations.

Print media are not the cheapest way to inform others about an event, but they are longer lasting than electronic media: It takes more effort and thought to throw out an invitation received in the mail than it does to hit the delete key on your computer.

146. *Useful Templates*

Why use templates?

Earlier on in the book we talked about a power page and the things you could put on it to keep track of extra client details before entering them into your CRM or contact files. The power page is an example of a useful template. You can create other templates that represent items such as your pipeline. The pipeline you see pictured at the end of the chapter is from Power Marketing International and is used by many companies around the world. Creating and using templates makes your life easier and facilitates sharing your expertise with others. Print some of your best ones and hand them out at events. Make sure your contact information is on all pages.

When you share a template, you are creating an opportunity to share your expertise and to gain the confidence of potential customers. They will want to get to know you better and learn more about what you do. Just make sure that you do not give away everything all at once—give them a teaser that is useful so that they will come back for more.

Whatever you decide to do to share some of your knowledge, be consistent with your message. Make sure that everything is trademarked so that you will get recognition when your ideas are shared with others whom you are not aware of. Watermark forms on the Web and ingrain your logo and contact information.

147. The Corporate Brochure's Power

Why use a professional brochure?

If you want to do business with anyone, you have to look the part. You would not likely show up to an initial meeting in a boardroom with torn jeans and a muscle shirt. On the contrary, you would likely dress up for the occasion and wear dress slacks and a businesslike shirt or blouse.

The same needs to be true for a business brochure. Besides the business card, the business brochure is your first step forward. The brochure tells the potential customer not only about your company through the content but also how you regard yourself in terms of professional design and print quality. If you produce your brochure on your home printer, it will show through whether you think it will or not. Professional print jobs use better quality paper and better quality inks. You should not have your brochure photocopied; you need to have it done properly.

This is not an advertisement for your local print shop; it is an advertisement for looking good from your first step forward. If your company does not look good in print, then the customer will wonder what kind of quality he is to expect from your work. I am not saying to go out and spend hundreds of dollars on design and printing; I am saying that you need to have a place in the budget to have it done right. It is much harder to re-attract a potential customer who was put off by inferior promotional materials than it is to convince the potential customer to use you in the first place. If you cannot afford a brochure, at least point potential customers to your Web site where the information is located.

Take a look at what your competitors are doing. If they have a really slick brochure, you can be guaranteed that they are getting greater opportunities for more business. Sometimes how you look is what counts. Who would you rather do business with, a poorly dressed slob or a neatly dressed professional?

148. *Power Pads*

What makes Power Pads
similar to the printed template?

The Power Pad is a template form that you can carry around with you when you visit clients. The Power Pad is a printed pad of paper that lists specific items you should record about the potential customer. Why is the Power Pad a template when you write so much information on it and transfer it to a computer program? By template in this instance, we mean a "form."

You have all filled out order forms, forms for getting refunds, and so on. Each of these forms requires the same information over and over again. We use forms to capture information, and when you create your Power Pad templates, you will actually be creating a handwritten form that can be later transferred to the computer. Forms help you to be more organized and also to make sure you get all the information that you need when in a meeting. A form will help you ask the right questions to fill in important information.

Creating your own template will make you think about what is important. It will also help you to discard some data as totally irrelevant to the business at hand. You should carefully think about what data to gather and then design your form (template) so that it is easy to use. I know I have filled out information on some forms and wondered why they would need to know some of the things they ask for. Make it easy on yourself and know what it is you need to have in order to get to the proposal.

Do not give yourself lots of work; only gather what you need now and what you can use in the future. Design your template to be practical and useful. You can even have a space that records what promo items you have given to this client or to your potential customer. It gives you an excuse to call them and create yet another touch point.

149. Giving Away Sample Work

Have you written a book or a white paper?
Give copies away for potential clients to read
and they will deem you the expert.

Event giveaways can cost you a fortune if they are not given out to your target audience. Plan them carefully around who is attending the event where you have a display. Also find out how many people are expected to attend, and what other people are giving away. If you can, talk to others putting up displays to find out what they will be using as promos. This way you are forewarned and forearmed.

At this point you can decide what will make you stand out from the crowd. Perhaps you will have your white papers printed with your card stapled on and a feedback form inside. When you give them away, ask the recipients to fill out the form or go to your Web site and add their comments. You will not get one hundred percent response, but those who are genuinely interested will take time to go to the site and fill out the comment form.

When at an event, you want to make sure you are remembered for the correct things. You do not want to be remembered for the candy you gave away or the door prize you sponsored. You want to be remembered for your expertise and the practical information you gave booth drop-bys. It is this quality that the person picking up your promo item will deem more important than the item itself.

If your information attracts attention, you can be assured that more people will flock to your booth to pick it up. Having said this, I must caution you that you will always get people at trade shows who are there only to pick up the goodies without taking time to find out anything about you or your business. You cannot avoid these people, but at least they tend to be in the minority.

Just remember, when you are at a trade show and giving out materials and promo items, that you are also after name recognition. Do not make it difficult for people to know who you are. Just make it obvious that you are the expert and your printed materials will serve to inform and educate them with no strings attached.

150. *The Power of a Book*

Why does nothing push your
expertise more than a book?

A book will push you farther along the path to being seen as an expert, for various reasons. First, the book will contain comments from others in the form of testimonials that create an aura of expertise around you. People tend to put more credence in what others say about you than in what you say about yourself. Second, a book means that you have put a lot of thought and effort into planning and expanding on your expertise. The book verifies that you really are the expert. Third, a book goes beyond your events and seminars; it is available to others who are far-flung in various parts of the country or the world. This scope even further emphasizes your expertise.

If you put on an event such as a seminar and place the title of your book in the advertising, you will likely obtain more attendees, and, even better, you will obtain more sales for your book. If you decide to write a book, you must remember that it does take a lot of hard work to research your topics and place them in an understandable format. It is not a project that many can complete in a short period of time. It will take perseverance and scheduled time to get it completed.

I use a well-tested formula for writing books (I have written over one hundred books, some of them in very technical subjects). Using a formula eases the writing process, but it still does not replace research and ability. You may find that hiring a ghostwriter or being coached by a professional will help you get there.

The important message here is that a book will substantiate who you are even if it is not published yet. If you do announce that you are in the process of writing a book, make sure you give a publication date that is realistic and that you can accomplish. Do not talk about or mention such an eventuality unless you are serious, as its failure to materialize may put your business relationships in jeopardy.

Checklists

Look at the main business card you use, is it memorable? Why or why not?

_____

_____

_____

_____

When did you issue your last press release? _____

Write a short headline that can be used for a press release for your most recent product or service.

_____

_____

_____

_____

What newspaper columns or magazine editorials and columns do you read most frequently?

_____

_____

_____

_____

_____

_____

Choose two items listed above and find out how to send in a comment or rebuttal and to whom.

_____

_____

What sample reports could you produce to send out free to potential customers?

_____

_____

_____

_____

What advertising promo items do you have today? _____

What advertising items do you think would benefit your company's exposure?

_____

_____

_____

_____

If you have a company brochure, how do you feel it gets the message across? (Is there a call to action?)

_____

_____

_____

_____

_____

_____

_____

_____

White Paper Format:

A white paper is generally 10 pages in length including the covers. The paper should contain the following information:

Page 1: Cover/title page displaying in large type the title of the paper and in smaller type the name of the author, the name of the company, and the date.

Page 2: Contains all copyright information.

Page 3: An Introduction to the company producing the paper, including a very brief description of the products or services offered, and a description of the contents of the paper.

Pages 4 to 8: The body of the paper. This should be written in a format that gives the reader at least seven major points.

Page 9: The conclusion

Page 10: Back cover. Could contain ordering information for additional papers, books, seminars, or similar items. This information should be brief and to the point. If you overdo this page, the paper will not get read.

If you keep your white paper very simple yet very informative, you may receive requests for more information.

The Sales Pipeline

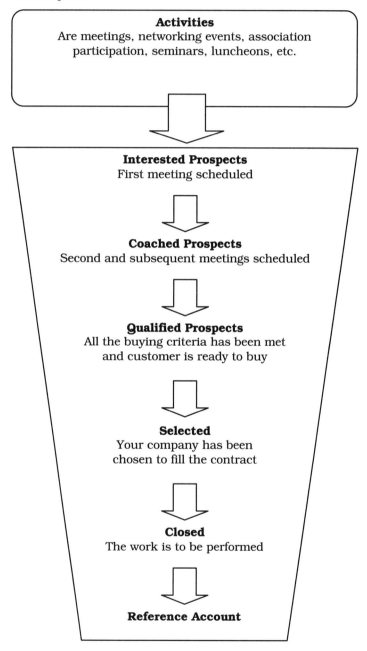

Activities
Are meetings, networking events, association participation, seminars, luncheons, etc.

Interested Prospects
First meeting scheduled

Coached Prospects
Second and subsequent meetings scheduled

Qualified Prospects
All the buying criteria has been met and customer is ready to buy

Selected
Your company has been chosen to fill the contract

Closed
The work is to be performed

Reference Account

Last Word

Networking is an art that will eventually lead to more business. You cannot take the process lightly; if you want to succeed you must constantly connect with others.

Every day you see people, talk to people, stand in lines, buy goods and services. Each one of the people you interact with could lead to more business. My husband is always talking to people in lines. Some people do not like it, but most of the time you can meet some really interesting individuals. The point of talking to strangers is to find out what they do. Do not talk about yourself—connect through their interests. If you don't find a business connection, at least you have become acquainted with another person in this world. If you find you have something in common, you may exchange business cards and perhaps do business in the future.

Networking should be an all-day activity and not just at leads exchange events, association meetings, and community picnics. You work with people every day: Try and get to know them better. You never know who is in their circle of influence. Your neighbors may work in an office where you are trying to get a connection, so may the people who are at your kids' soccer game. You never know where the next good lead will appear.

NOTES

Resource Guide

The following lists are of resources you can use to increase you networking activity. The books listed will allow you to delve deeper into some of the areas discussed in this book.

NOTES

Books

Best Practices: Building Your Business with Customer-Focused Solutions
by Arthur Andersen, Charles Ketteman, Robert Heibeler,
Thomas B. Kelly
ISBN: 068484804X

Customer Centered Growth: Five Proven Strategies for Building Competitive Advantage
by Richard Whiteley, Diane Hessan
ISBN: 0201154935

The Customer Driven Company: Moving from Talk to Action
by Richard C. Whiteley
ISBN: 0201608138

Effective Listening Skills
by Art James, Dennis Kratz
ISBN 0786301228

Listening: The Forgotten Skill : A Self-Teaching Guide
By Madelyn Burley-Allen
ISBN: 0471015873

Listen Up: How to Improve Relationships, Reduce Stress, and Be More Productive by Using the Power of Listening
by Larry Barker, Ph.D., Kittie W. Watson, Ph.D.
ISBN: 0312242654

The Good Listener
by James E. Sullivan
ISBN: 0877939438

Networking Magic: Find the Best—from Doctors, Lawyers, and Accountants to Homes, Schools, and Jobs
by Rick Frishman, Jill Lublin, Mark Steisel
ISBN: 1593370202

Dig Your Well Before You're Thirsty : The Only Networking Book You'll Ever Need
by Harvey Mackay
ISBN: 0385485468

The Networking Survival Guide: Get the Success You Want by Tapping Into the People You Know
by Diane Darling
ISBN: 0071409998

Smooth Selling
By Elinor Stutz
ISBN: 0-9762942-0-6

Stepping Into Greatness: Success Is Up to YOU!
by Daniel Gutierrez
Prepublication

Nonstop Networking: How to Improve Your Life, Luck, and Career
by Andrea R. Nierenberg
ISBN: 1892123924

Breakthrough Networking: Building Relationships That Last, Second
Edition
by Lillian D. Bjorseth
ISBN: 0964883937

Supernetworking: Reach the Right People, Build Your Career Network, and Land Your Dream Job—Now
by Michael Salmon
ISBN: 1564147002

So You'd Like to . . . Get What You Want in Life Using the Magic of Networking
A guide by Rick Frishman

How Full Is Your Bucket? Positive Strategies for Work and Life
by Tom Rath, Donald O. Clifton
ISBN: 1595620036

Here's My Card: How to Network Using Your Business Card to Actually Create More Business
by Bob Popyk
ISBN: 1580631134

Now, Discover Your Strengths
by Marcus Buckingham, Donald O. Clifton
ISBN: 0743201140

Leads Exchanges

LeadsEvents.com
The Leads Events Web site was designed to list events that are happening throughout the U.S. and sometimes beyond. This site is membership based and groups can list their events. The site has valuable information that should not be missed. For more information visit www.leadsevents.com

BNI
BNI (Business Network International) is a business and professional networking organization that offers members the opportunity to share ideas, contacts, and, most importantly, referrals. BNI has chapters in many countries. For more information visit www.bni.com

B2B Power Exchange
B2B Power Exchange was started by Leadgenaires in order to obtain more clients for their growing marketing business. The group is based in the San Francisco Bay Area and emphasizes a business to business structure. Members of this group are dedicated to doing business with one another and to give referrals and introductions to their own networks. There are four operating groups. For more information visit www.B2BPowerExchange.com

LeTip
LeTip International, Inc., is a professional organization of men and women dedicated to the highest standards of competence and service. The primary purpose is to give and receive qualified business tips or leads. Members will, at all times, maintain the highest professional integrity. Each business category is represented by one member, and conflicts of interest are disallowed. For more information visit www.letip.com

NFP
NFP (Networking for Professionals) makes business networking easy by connecting you with successful professionals who can best help grow your business, improve your client base, and advance your career. For more information visit
www.networkingforprofessionals.com

B2B Gathering
B2B Gathering is a privately held networking organization with groups throughout the San Francisco Bay Area that are growing rapidly. The emphasis is to connect business people to further their business. For more information visit www.b2bgathering.com

Associations

IMC (Institute of Management Consultants)
IMC USA is the professional association and certifying body dedicated to promoting excellence and ethics in management consulting. The IMC USA mission is to provide certification, education, and professional resources to management consultants. IMC USA awards the profession's internationally recognized certification, the CMC (Certified Management Consultant), an acknowledgment of extensive experience, peer reviews, client audits, and adherence to the IMC USA Code of Ethics. IMC USA benefits include professional development and networking through its 23 U.S. chapters. Website: www.imcusa.org. Look up the Northern California Chapter, to connect with other consultants, at www.imcnorcal.org

ASTD (American Society of Training and Development)
ASTD is the world's largest association dedicated to workplace learning and performance professionals. ASTD's 70,000 members and associates come from more than 100 countries and thousands of organizations—multinational corporations, medium-sized and small businesses, government, academia, consulting firms, and product and service suppliers. For more information visit www.astd.org

NHRA (National Human Resources Association)
Established in 1951, NHRA is a network of local affiliates focused on advancing the development of human resource professionals. Through programs and services offered across the country, NHRA strives to support human resources professionals throughout their career life cycle—from intern to executive—as human resources leads the way for change in today's businesses. The mission of the NHRA Board is to serve and support NHRA affiliates in providing networking forums and professional development for their members. For more information visit www.nhra.org

Directory of Associations
Associations are a powerful resource for building and expanding networking and business opportunities, finding jobs, evaluating goods and services, and researching trends or publications. This database puts you in direct contact with these organizations. For more information visit www.marketingsource.com

Networking Opportunities

Chambers of Commerce
Chambers of Commerce will provide you with many networking and business building opportunities. Almost every community has a Chamber and most states have an umbrella organization to which the state's Chambers belong. The best way to find out about your local Chamber of Commerce is to do an internet search or visit your local library.

Try the California Chamber of Commerce to get a listing of Chambers in California. You can also go the United States Chamber of Commerce to find out which states have Chambers and how to contact them.

eBig
eBig is an organization in California that boasts over 10,000 members. These members belong to SIGs (special interest groups) that are related to technology. The group is always looking for individuals to form additional SIGs and to attend their many events. For more information visit www.eBIG.org

LinkedIn
LinkedIn is an online network community. This community has you invite your contacts to join the network. They in turn become members of your personal network. Your contacts can then form their own network, which you can see from your link to them. The potential ring of contacts is almost limitless. You can do searches and find people you want to be introduced to and follow the chain of links to get that introduction. If you utilize the service, it can aid you in generating a lot of business. Visit: www.linkedin.com—join and request a link to Bette Daoust.

Ryze
Ryze helps you expand your business network. Make quality business contacts; reconnect with friends (you probably know people in here already); help your company make deals through Ryze members. Build your network BEFORE you need it! Ryze has a free service but also provides a paid component. For more information visit: www.ryze.com

Yahoo groups
Yahoo provides many special interest groups and other opportunities to connect with others on the Web. Visit groups.yahoo.com and create your own i.d. and password to join most of the listings.

Google groups

Google has its beta groups forum up and running. To try it out, visit groups-beta.google.com. This site is starting to see some action and is well worth exploring.

Monster Network

Monster has started its own version of networking for those seeking employment. As an offshoot of this service, people can connect with each other to do business even after they have found employment. For more information visit: www.monster.com

Many other networking opportunities are available in almost every city in the world. If you contact your local Chamber, they can usually give you enough information to connect with at least one group. You may also want to try an Internet search for other networking opportunities.

Service Organizations

Rotary
Rotary is a service organization that celebrated its centennial in 2005. This organization has a club in almost every city in the U.S. and is in almost every country of the world. If you are interested in being involved in a service organization, most of the members of Rotary give time and money to worthwhile projects that are local, regional, and international. For a club near you visit www.rotary.org

Kiwanis
Kiwanis is an international service organization that provides service and money to the community and beyond. For more information visit www.kiwanis.org

Lions
Lions clubs are found in most cities and towns in North America and beyond. Lions clubs do service projects equal to other organizations'. For more information visit www.lionsclubs.org

There are many other service organizations in most communities. The three listed here are simply the largest. Visit your local library, Chamber of Commerce, or downtown association to get a list of clubs available in your area.

NOTES

Index

Networking
The Seminar

This seminar is part of the Blueprints for Success series of books for business. The impetus behind the series was to provide exactly what I wished had been available when I started my first business. These books are meant to be a guide for those who are not quite sure of how to start. And for those veterans in the business world, this book offers a new perspective on old procedures and new ones. In a nutshell, it is the business world through my eyes and how these methods worked for me. I have taught these methods to many people and to my children who have told me numerous times that they appreciated how I view the world of business and taught them to do the same. This book may not be for everyone but I think that everyone should have one. The methods and tips in this book are a valuable part of business and should be part of your business library.

Upcoming titles in the Blueprints for Success series include:
Blueprints for Success - eMarketing
Blueprints for Success - Leadership
Blueprints for Success - Branding Yourself
Blueprints for Success - Discovery Selling
Blueprints for Success - Workforce Mobility
Blueprints for Success - Publicity
Blueprints for Success - Marketing

Interested in being one of our authors? Send an email with your proposal to author@blueprintbooks.com

**Be sure to look for additional titles on our website:
www.BlueprintBooks.com**

Quick Order Form

Blueprint Books
Blueprints for Success

Fax Orders: 800-605-2914

Telephone Orders: Call 800-605-2913 toll free.
                             Have your credit card ready.

Email Orders: orders@BlueprintBooks.com

Postal Orders: Blueprint Books
                              PO Box 10757,
                              Pleasanton, CA 94588 USA

Please send the following books, discs or reports. I understand that I may return any of them for a full refund-for any reason, no questions asked.

_____

_____

Please send more FREE information on:

[ ] Other books [ ] Speaking/Seminars [ ] Consulting

Name: _____
Address: _____
            City: _____ State: _____ Zip: _____
Telephone: _____
Email address: _____

Sales tax: Please add 8.75% for products shipped to California addresses.

Shipping by Air: US $5.00 for the first book and $3.00 for each additional product.

International: $10 for first book or disk; $6.00 for each additional product (estimate).

Payment: [ ] Check   [ ] Credit Card:
              [ ] Visa [ ] MasterCard   [ ] American Express

Card Number: _____

Name on card: _____
Expiration Date: ___/_____ (month/year)